Madeira

by Christopher Catling

Christopher Catling has written more than 30 travel guides. He is a regular contributor to travel magazines on the Internet and in print. His books on London, Florence, Venice and Amsterdam are inspired by a keen interest in art and architecture, while his love of the countryside is reflected in guides to Madeira, Umbria and Crete.

Above: a walker on the Levada do Risco footpath enjoys the view

AA Publishing

Abovè: *the 17th-century fortress guarding Funchal's harbour*

Written by Christopher Catling

First published 1998
Reprinted April 1999; Feb and Aug 2000
Reprinted 2001. Information verified and updated. Reprinted May 2002
Reprinted Feb 2003, Reprinted Jan 2004, May 2004

© Automobile Association Developments Limited 1998, 2001
Maps © Automobile Association Developments Limited 1998, 2001

Published by AA Publishing, a trading name of Automobile Association Developments Limited, whose registered office is Millstream, Maidenhead Road, Windsor, Berkshire SL4 5GD. Registered number 1878835.

Automobile Association Developments Limited retains the copyright in the original edition © 1998 and in all subsequent editions, reprints and amendments

A CIP catalogue record for this book is available from the British Library.

ISBN 0 7495 1919 3

A02230

Colour separation: Pace Colour, Southampton
Printed and bound in Italy by Printer Trento S.r.l.

Find out more about AA Publishing and the wide range of services the AA provides by visiting our web site at www.theAA.com

Contents

About this Book

This book is divided into five sections to cover the most important aspects of your visit to Madeira.

Viewing Madeira pages 5–14
An introduction to Madeira by the author.
Madeira's Features
Essence of Madeira
The Shaping of Madeira
Peace and Quiet
Madeira's Famous

Top Ten pages 15–26
The author's choice of the Top Ten places to see in Madeira, listed in alphabetical order, each with practical information.

What to See pages 27–90
The five main areas of Madeira, each with its own brief introduction and an alphabetical listing of the main attractions.
Practical information
Snippets of 'Did you know…' information
6 suggested walks
4 suggested tours
2 features

Where To… pages 91–116
Detailed listings of the best places to eat, stay, shop, take the children and be entertained.

Practical Matters pages 117–24
A highly visual section containing essential travel information.

Maps
All map references are to the individual maps found in the What to See section of this guide.
For example, Calheta has the reference
🗺 48B2 – indicating the page on which the map is located and the grid square in which the town is to be found.
A list of the maps that have been used in this travel guide can be found in the index.

Prices
Where appropriate, an indication of the cost of an establishment is given by £ signs:
£££ denotes higher prices, **££** denotes average prices, while **£** denotes lower charges.

Star Ratings
Most of the places described in this book have been given a separate rating:
✪✪✪   Do not miss
✪✪   Highly recommended
✪   Worth seeing

Viewing
Madeira

Above: *Penha de Águia (Eagle Rock) looms over the Ametade valley*
Right: *making a wicker chair at Camacha*

Christopher Catling's Madeira

Echoes of Other Worlds
With its mild and balmy climate, its flowers and its terraced hillsides, Madeira reminds some visitors of Bali or the Philippines. Others find Funchal, the island capital, reminiscent of towns in Brazil, Venezuela or Colombia, with its colonial-style town houses and elegant balconies dripping with flowers.

A flower-seller in Madeiran costume in Funchal's cathedral square

Madeira has never quite lost its image of being an island retreat for those in delicate health, a place where the bankrupt old nobility of Europe could flee to escape their debts, or a retirement home for impoverished former colonial servants. Young travellers turn up their noses at the thought of a destination with no beaches, and no nightlife: Madeira is definitely not a ravers' paradise.

It is, however, one of Europe's most intriguing destinations. The island's mountainous volcanic landscape is carved into scores of deep valleys and ravines, clothed in the luxuriant vegetation that thrives in the frost-free climate. Hundreds of miles of footpaths run alongside the ingenious network of irrigation canals (called *levadas*), bringing water from the wet side of the island to the sunny but drier south. Easy to follow, these paths lead you deep into the quiet rural heart of the island, where the agriculture and way of life has hardly caught up with the industrial era.

Flowers are Madeira's other main attraction; a whole week can be filled visiting its parks and gardens. Colourful species introduced from South Africa, South America and Asia flourish in every rural front garden and on every urban balcony. Practically every roadside on the island has been colonised by amaryllis, poinsettias, agaves and bird-of-paradise plants, and the markets are full of colourful orchids and cut flowers, which you can buy to take home.

For those of us who know and love this island, the walks, the landscapes and the beautiful verdant countryside, combined with the ever-friendly people and appetising food, make Madeira a place of immense appeal.

Madeira's Features

Geography
- Set in the eastern Atlantic, the island of Madeira lies roughly 1,000km from Lisbon and 600km from Morocco, the nearest mainland.
- Madeira measures 54km by 23km (741sq km), and has a population of 300,000.
- Madeira's nearest neighbour is the island of Porto Santo (population 5,000), which lies 37km to the northeast. Measuring just 106sq km, the island is blessed with a magnificent 11km sweep of sandy beach.
- Also part of the Madeiran archipelago are two groups of uninhabited islands the three Ilhas Desertas (Desert Isles), which are situated 10km to the southeast of Madeira, and the Ilhas Selvagens (Savage Isles), which lie 216km to the south.

Landscape
- Madeira is the product of volcanic eruptions that took place some 20 million years ago. Volcanic peaks are a major feature of the island, several of them rising to more than 1,800m.
- Christopher Columbus described Madeira to Queen Isabella of Spain by crumpling up a piece of paper: apart from the southern coastal plain, the mountainous island is carved into myriad deep valleys and ravines.
- Driving distances are greatly magnified by the steep terrain, necessitating slow progress along the tortuous zig-zagging roads.

Climate
- Madeira's climate is sub-tropical: the southerly latitude ensures warm, frost-free winters and cooling Atlantic winds take the edge off the intense heat of summer.
- Atlantic fronts drop rain on the north side of the island, while the south side remains dry and sunny for much of the year.

Deep green valleys and ravines characterise Madeira's interior

Exports
Madeira's fortune was built on sugar production in the 15th to 17th centuries, but the bubble burst when cheap Caribbean sugar flooded the European market. The production of Madeira wine sustained the island in the 18th and 19th centuries. Today, tourism is the biggest revenue earner, and bananas, grown in the island's sunny south, compete with wine as the most valuable export.

7

Essence of Madeira

Landscape and climate combine on Madeira to create an island of all-year-round appeal. In winter, while northern Europe shivers, southerly Madeira is basking in balmy sunshine. In summer, while searing heat turns much of southern Europe arid, the island remains a green semi-tropical paradise, the air heavy with the scent of flowers. To travel around Madeira is to encounter breathtaking views at every turn, whether sheer rock cliffs battered by Atlantic waves, burnt volcanic rocks lit gold by the setting sun, or valleys carved into tiny fields, forming a patchwork of stepped terraces.

Right: *Monte toboggan drivers are easily identified by their striking costumes*
Below: *festive flutters in Caniçal*

THE 10 ESSENTIALS

If you only have a short time on Madeira, or would like to gain a rounded picture of the island, be sure to experience the following highlights.

• **Spend a day in Funchal** (➤ 30), with its mosaic-patterned streets, its embroidery shops and its elegant town houses.

• **Step back in time** on a visit to the Adegas de São Francisco wine lodge (➤ 16) in Funchal, to learn all about the history of Madeira wine production.

• **Go for dinner in Funchal's Zona Velha** (Old Town, ➤ 26) and listen to the plaintive and haunting sound

Left: *mosaics decorate Funchal's pavements*
Centre: *dinner al fresco in the Zona Velha (Old Town)*
Below: *exotic Canna lilies bloom in Blandy's Garden*

of Portuguese *fado* music.

• **Spend a night** in the hotel on top of Pico do Arieiro (➤ 23), Madeira's third highest peak, to enjoy the scintillating colours of the Madeiran sunset, or to wonder at the mass of stars in the crystal-clear night sky.

• **Visit the Quinta do Palheiro Ferreiro** (➤ 24), also known as Blandy's Garden, to see the flowers and shrubs of several continents artfully blended to create a fascinating garden.

• **Take a walk** along a *levada* (irrigation canal), penetrating deep into the peaceful heart of the Madeiran countryside.

• **Drive from São Vicente to Porto Moniz** along the scenically spectacular northern coast of Madeira, through rock-cut tunnels and beneath waterfalls.

• **Join in a village festivity** for the fun of noisy fireworks and to taste *espetada* (beef kebabs) cooked over an open wood fire.

• **Take a trip to Curral das Freiras** (➤ 18) to marvel at the scenic beauty of this hidden valley at the island's heart.

• **Visit the Whaling Museum** (➤ 77) at Caniçal to learn about plans to provide protection for these captivating sea mammals, and loiter on the nearby beach to watch the fishermen land their catch or work on their boats.

The Shaping of Madeira

20 million BC
Madeira is formed through volcanic eruptions.

1.7 million BC
The Madeiran volcanoes become extinct, the lava cools and storms erode the weaker rocks to create deep valleys and ravines. Vegetation cloaks the island from seaborne seeds.

AD 100
Pliny mentions the Madeiran archipelago in his *Natural History* (AD 77), calling them the 'Purple Islands' after the reddish-purple dye obtained from the sap of the island's dragon trees.

1351
The Medici Map, now in the Laurentian Library in Florence, depicts three islands off the African coast named Porto Santo, Deserta and Isola de Lolegname (Italian for Wooded Isle).

1370s
An English merchant called Robert Machin is shipwrecked on Madeira with his lover, Anne of Hereford. Madeira's second largest town – Machico – was later founded on the spot where Anne died and, it is said, named in the couple's honour.

1418
João Gonçalves Zarco is blown out to sea by a storm while exploring the west coast of Africa. Having found a safe anchorage off Porto Santo, he returns to Lisbon to report his sighting of a mist- and wood-covered island on the horizon.

1419
Prince Henry the Navigator sends a fleet, headed by Zarco, to explore these islands further. Zarco establishes a base in Porto Santo.

1420
Zarco lands on Madeira (Wooded) and claims it for Portugal. The island is set alight as the fastest way of clearing land for settlement.

1425
Madeira is officially declared a province of Portugal. Zarco, appointed governor of the western half of the island, founds Funchal; Tristão Vaz, governor of the east, founds the island's second city, Machico; and Bartolomeu Perestrelo colonises Porto Santo.

1452
Madeira's sub-tropical climate and fertile volcanic soils prove ideal for sugar cultivation; slaves are imported from Africa and the Canary Islands to create terraced fields, dig irrigation channels and work the fields.

1478
Christopher Columbus visits Madeira, which has now become a major sugar producer.

Prince Henry, who sent Zarco to claim Madeira

Catherine Queen of Charles II.
From an Original by Sir Peter Lely.

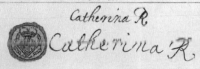

Catherine of Braganza,
Charles II's queen

1891
Reid's Hotel opens its doors, catering for the increasing number of wealthy visitors over-wintering in Madeira.

1964
Madeira's isolation ends with the opening of Santa Catarina airport.

1974
Portugal becomes a democracy after soldiers overthrow the post-war dictatorship, with flowers in their gun-barrels to symbolise their peaceful intentions.

1976
Madeira becomes an autonomous region, with its own parliament.

1986
Portugal's European Union membership releases development funds for improving Madeira's infrastructure, bringing electricity and roads to remote rural communities.

1997
The opening of the island's new south-coast expressway transforms transport on the island. Villages that were once half a day's travel from the capital can now be reached in half an hour.

1514
According to the first official census, Madeira now has 5,000 inhabitants (excluding slaves) and Funchal is Portugal's third most populous city, after Lisbon and Porto.

1566
Some 1,000 French pirates raid Funchal, the capital, killing the governor and 250 Madeirans. Mansions and churches are looted in the worst of several such raids on the island.

1580
Madeira comes under Spanish rule after Philip II conquers Portugal.

1640
The Portuguese revolt against Spanish rule and regain independence under King João IV.

1662
By marrying Catherine of Braganza, Charles II gains trading concessions for English merchants, which paved the way for their eventual domination of the Madeira wine trade.

1852
After mildew devastates the island's vineyards, new, more resilient vine varieties are planted, laying the foundations of the modern Madeira wine industry.

11

Peace & Quiet

On Madeira you can escape quickly and easily from the bustle of modern life by walking alongside the island's extensive network of irrigation canals. Called *levadas*, these watercourses link village to village and penetrate deep into the mountainous heart of the island. *Levadas* follow the island's contours, falling with an almost imperceptible gradient so it is possible to walk for miles on level paths, enjoying Madeira's exhilarating landscapes with none of the physical effort normally associated with mountain climbing. Along the route you will encounter shady eucalyptus forest, fragrant with menthol, sun-dappled clearings where butterflies feed, banks of wild hydrangeas and amaryllis, rural farms and orchards, rock-cut tunnels and waterfalls.

The Work of Centuries

Levadas are as old as the earliest settlement on Madeira. The first rock-cut irrigation canals were dug in the 15th century using slave and convict labour. Over the centuries, more and more canals were dug to distribute water from the upland areas, where rainfall is plentiful, to the banana plantations, vineyards and terraced fields of the sunny south side of Madeira. Today, the canal network extends to more than 2,150km; it is fed by naturally occurring springs and by purpose-built reservoirs. As well as irrigating the fields, the *levadas* supply water to several of the island's electricity-generating power stations.

Maintaining the *levadas* is the task of the *levadeiro*, who patrols a stretch of watercourse, clearing landslips and fallen debris. He also operates the sluices that channel the water to different farms along the route according to a pre-arranged timetable.

Top: *Banana plantations irrigated by* levadas
Above: *The watercourses create miles of footpath*

Levada Walking

Most *levadas* are easy to find and follow, but proper precautions should still be taken. Some *levadas* pass through long tunnels, so you need to take a torch with plenty of battery power. Many paths cross aqueducts or cling to steep hillsides with a sheer drop to one or both sides: anyone who suffers from vertigo should beware. Comfortable walking shoes will prevent blisters, and they need to be slip-proof to avoid accidents on wet and mossy paths. Be prepared for all types of weather, ranging from a sudden shower to blistering sun.

If you want to sample a *levada*, try one of the short and easy-to-follow walks detailed in this book (see the Rabaçal route, ➤ 55, or the Balcões walk, ➤ 66). Alternatively, you can join a guided tour led by a knowledgeable local guide (further details from the tourist office in Funchal or through travel agencies on the island).

Once you have found your feet you can set off on your own, perhaps guided by John and Pat Underwood's *Landscapes of Madeira* (published by Sunflower Books; copies can be bought at the Funchal tourist office and in most bookshops on Madeira). The book details over 80 walks of different length and character: whichever you choose, you can be sure that the gentle sound of running water will accompany your every step, and that exhilarating views are guaranteed.

Basking lizards may be seen adorning a wall or rock

Lizard Lore

As you walk round the Madeiran countryside, sudden rustlings in the undergrowth may take you by surprise. The chances are that, if the noise does not come from a grazing goat, it is caused by one of the island's shy but ubiquitous lizards. Varying in colour from basalt black to bright green, they can grow up to 17cm in length. Farmers regard them as a mixed blessing: though they can help to keep down pests, such as mosquitoes and slugs, they also like to feed on the grapes and soft fruit growing in the island's vineyards and orchards.

Madeira's Famous

Christopher Columbus

Working as a buyer for a group of Lisbon-based sugar merchants, Christopher Columbus (1451–1506) visited

Madeira on three separate occasions. On his first visit, in 1478, he sought out the company of his compatriot Bartolomeu Perestrelo, the Genova-born governor of the island of Porto Santo. Not long after, he married Dona Filipa Moniz, Perestrelo's daughter. Their child, Diego, was born in 1479, but Dona Filipa died in 1480. During his stay on Porto Santo, Columbus became convinced by the vegetation washed up on the island's shores that there must be land beyond the western horizon. Twelve years later he persuaded the Castilian monarchs, Ferdinand and Isabella, to fund the voyage that proved his hunch to be correct.

Christopher Columbus and his family lived for a time on Porto Santo

Napoleon Bonaparte

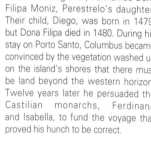

The emperor Napoleon (1769–1821) was an involuntary visitor to Madeira in 1815, when the ship carrying him to exile on St Helena moored in Funchal harbour. The British Consul, Henry Veitch, went on board and gave the vanquished emperor gifts of fruit and books. Veitch was subsequently dismissed from his post for addressing Napoleon as 'Your Majesty', though Lord Palmerston later reinstated him. Napoleon is said to have ordered a barrel of Madeira wine which he paid for with some gold coins that were later to be placed ceremoniously under the foundation stone of the island's neoclassical English Church, completed in 1822.

Winston Churchill

Napoleon never drank his barrel of Madeira. Instead it was returned to the island in 1822, where it continued to mature. More than a century later, in 1950, Winston Churchill (1874–1965) chose to spend a holiday here, painting the coastal scenery around Câmara de Lobos (► 62) and enjoying the hospitality at the elegant Reid's Hotel. At a dinner given in his honour, he was presented with a bottle of 'the Napoleon Madeira'. Sharing this with his fellow guests, he reminded them that 'when this wine was made, Marie Antoinette was still alive'.

Last Resting Place
Buried in a plain black coffin in Monte church is the Emperor Charles I (1887–1922), last of the Austro-Hungarian Habsburg emperors. Charles succeeded at the death of his great uncle, Franz Joseph, in 1916, but was deposed at the end of World War I. After deportation to Switzerland he chose to spend the rest of his brief life in exile on Madeira.

Top Ten

Above: *Madeira wine ranges
from dry to raisin-sweet*
Right: *a Monte toboggan driver
waiting for passengers*

1
Adegas de São Francisco

32B2

Avenida Arriaga 28, Funchal

740 110

Guided tours: Mon–Fri 10:30, 3:30, Sat 11. Closed Sun, public hols

Theatre café (£) opposite

Avenida Arriaga 16

Few

Moderate

Jardim de Santa Catarina (➤ 36), Museu Fortaleza (➤ 38)

Visit a wine lodge set in a medieval monastery to sample Madeira and learn how it is produced.

To step from the bustle of Funchal's main street into the calm courtyards of the Adegas de São Francisco (St Francis Wine Lodge) is to enter a world where time has a different meaning. Here, on payment of a fairly substantial sum, you can buy wines that were bottled in the 1860s, while upstairs, slowly maturing in huge barrels of Brazilian satinwood and American oak, are wines that nobody living today is likely to taste. As Churchill said, 'to drink Madeira is to sip history with every glass'.

The lodge, with its romantic timber buildings and wisteria-hung balconies, started life as the monastery of St Francis and was converted to its present use in 1834. At that time, Madeira wines were still being sent on board ship to the equator and back in the belief that the rocking motion improved the wine. The production process was revolutionised by the accidental discovery that Madeira's unique quality comes not from motion but from gentle heating. Now the wine is 'cooked' in vast vats using the warmth of the sun, boosted when necessary by the heat from hot water pipes. All this becomes clear as you tour the cobbled yard to see ancient wooden presses and leather-bound wine ledgers, learn the subtle arts of the wine blender and visit the warming rooms, with their deliciously heady smell of old wood and wine. Scents such as these are a prelude to the pleasures to come as you head for the sampling that concludes this popular tour, which takes place in a room with delightful murals painted in 1922 by Max Romer.

Wine barrels in the courtyard of the Adegas de São Francisco

2
Cabo Girão

The towering cliff face of Cabo Girão can be viewed from a boat or from the dizzy heights of its cliff-top balcony.

Cabo Girão is not quite Europe's highest sea cliff – it is beaten into second place by a Norwegian competitor – but at 580m it is impressive enough. Girão means 'turning', an apt description of the vertiginous effect of looking down to the sea from the cliff top. In fact, it is said that the name dates from Zarco's first voyage of discovery when he set out to explore the Madeiran coast in 1420. His diary vividly describes sailing 'towards a dark, stupendous object... abode of demons and evil spirits'. Deciding to venture no further, Zarco turned back at this point to seek a safe anchorage at what is now the fishing port of Câmara de Lobos (► 62).

For a different view of Cabo Girão you can retrace Zarco's voyage by taking a boat excursion along Madeira's southern coast. Numerous companies offer tours from Funchal, and you can either book direct by visiting the marina, or through hotels and travel agents. Half-day tours go as far west as Ponta do Sol (► 52), and most operators anchor off Cabo Girão so that you can dive off the boat and swim in the clean, warm waters. One company, Turispeca (see side panel), also offers fishing trips.

Whether you choose to view Cabo Girão from above or below, look out for the tiny terraces cut into the cliff face, where brave and hardy farmers cultivate vines on pocket-handkerchief-sized plots, taking advantage of the warmth stored in these south facing rocks.

Looking towards the imposing mass of Cabo Girão

✚ 60B1

✉ 22km west of Funchal, and 10km west of Câmara de Lobos

🍴 Snack bar (£) alongside the viewing platform

🚌 Bus 154 from Funchal

🛥 Details of boat excursions from the tourist office in Funchal, Avenida Arriaga 16 (☎ 229 057) or through companies based in the yacht marina, such as Turispeca (☎ 231 063) and Costa do Sol (☎ 238 538)

♿ Few

↔ Câmara de Lobos (► 62)

3
Curral das Freiras

✝ 60B2

✉ 20km northwest of Funchal

🍴 Nuns' Valley Restaurant (£) in the centre of the village

🚌 Bus 81 from Funchal

♿ None

✋ Free

❓ Sun is market day

This secret valley, known as the Nuns' Corral (or Refuge), is hidden among the peaks of Madeira's central mountain range.

Only with mild exaggeration did H N Coleridge, nephew of the poet, describe Curral das Freiras (the name literally means Nuns' Corral) as 'one of the great sights of the world'. The majestic peaks that encircle the village certainly invite such claims, though quiet contemplation of the views can sometimes be difficult because of the sheer number of visitors in high season. If you enjoy bustle, go to Curral das Freiras on a Sunday, when a lively market spreads through the network of streets around the parish church. If not, the best way to find relative solitude is to walk into the village along the old zig-zag path that starts on the left as you emerge from the first of the modern road tunnels leading to the village (taxi drivers know this path and will drop you here if requested).

Until 1959, this grassy path was the only way in and out of the village. Its impregnability was the reason why the nuns of Santa Clara Convent (► 32) fled here in 1566 to escape from piratical raids on Funchal. A first glimpse of the hidden valley is to be had from the lookout point high above the village, signposted Eira do Serrado (Eagle's Nest). From here, the village far below seems to sit in the bowl of a vast crater, surrounded by sheer cliffs rising to jagged peaks. The view is not quite so enthralling from the bottom looking up, but there are other compensations: bars in Curral das Freiras sell the local speciality, a delicious chestnut-flavoured liqueur called *licor de castanha*.

Above and right: two dramatic views of the secretive Curral das Freiras valley from the well-named Eagle's Nest lookout point

18

4

Mercado dos Lavradores, Funchal

The covered market in Funchal is a cornucopia of colourful island produce, a great place to shop for fruit, flowers and souvenirs.

✚ 33C2

✉ Rua Dr Fernão Ornelas

🕐 Mon–Thu 7–4, Fri 7–8, Sat 7–3. Closed Sun

🍴 Many stalls selling snacks, plus bars and pavement cafés in the nearby Zona Velha

♿ None

↔ Zona Velha (➤ 26)

The Mercado dos Lavradores (Workers' Market) was built in the 1930s as a producers' market, where island farmers and fishermen could bring their produce for sale direct to the public. Now professional retailers predominate, but the original spirit prevails on Friday, as farmers from the remotest corners of Madeira descend on Funchal in loaded-down pick-up trucks.

Flower-sellers in traditional island costume have colonised the entrance to the market. Their stalls sell keenly priced cut flowers and bulbs – tubs full of amaryllis bulbs, freshly dug and smelling of earth, or delicate orchid blooms might tempt you to buy a souvenir of the island's horticultural richness.

Strelitzias (birds of paradise) are among the many exotic blooms on sale at the market

In the fish hall, there are scenes to turn the stomach. If the razor-sharp teeth and large staring eyes of the scabbard fish do not give you nightmares, the sight of huge tuna fish being gutted and filleted may well.

For pleasanter sights and fragrances, head for the upper floor, with its lavish displays of seasonal fruit and vegetables. The stallholders will seek to convince you that their fruits are the best by proffering a free sample on the end of a long knife. If you are self-catering on Madeira, you could do worse than come here to buy good fresh food, and if you are not, then just come here to enjoy the bustle.

5

The Monte Toboggan Ride

The quintessential Madeira experience is to slide in a metal-shod toboggan down the steep cobbled streets linking Monte to Funchal.

Hold on for a thrilling and unusual ride!

Was Ernest Hemingway being ironic when he described the Monte toboggan ride as one of the most exhilarating experiences of his life? The only way to find out is to try it for yourself by heading up to the hill town of Monte, high above Funchal. Here you can join the line of apprehensive travellers queuing to slide back down to the capital in a wicker basket mounted on polished metal runners. Two toboggan drivers, wearing rubber-soled boots for grip, will push and steer you over the bumpy cobbles and ensure that you do not come to grief as you negotiate sharp bends.

The 4km trip to Funchal will last about 20 minutes (alternatively, you can take the 10-minute trip to Livramento). Some visitors consider this brief but unique journey to be the highlight of their visit to Madeira – others consider it overpriced hype (as well as the price of the ride, you will be expected to tip the toboggan drivers, and pay for the souvenir photographs that are taken as you descend and presented to you at the journey's end).

➕ 61D1

✉ Toboggan rides start from the foot of the steps of Nossa Senhora do Monte church

🕐 Toboggan rides are available daily, 9–dusk

🍴 Café (£) frequented by toboggan drivers alongside church steps

🚌 Town bus 20 or Teleféricos da Madeiras (➤ 111)

✋ Expensive

↔ Monte (➤ 64)

6
Museu de Arte Sacra, Funchal

✝ 32B2

✉ Rua do Bispo 21

☎ 228 900

🕐 Tue–Sat 10–12:30, 2–5:30, Sun 10–1. Closed Mon, public hols

Enjoy masterpieces of Flemish art, paid for by Madeira's highly profitable sugar trade with northern Europe.

Funchal's Sacred Art Museum is housed in the former bishop's palace, built in 1600 and given its gracious cobbled courtyard and entrance staircase when the building was remodelled between 1748 and 1757. Displayed on the first floor is a collection of ancient religious vestments, silverware and statuary collected from remote churches all over Madeira. Some of these objects date to the earliest years of the island's colonisation, including the intricately decorated processional cross donated to Funchal Cathedral by the Portuguese King Manuel I, who reigned from 1490 to 1520.

The best of the museum's treasures are displayed on the upper floor. Here you can enjoy the naturalism and human pathos of several beautiful painted wooden statues of the Virgin and Child, as well as the warm colours of several fine Flemish masterpieces. For many years it was not known who painted these remarkable pictures of the Nativity, the Crucifixion and of various saints. By comparison with

Madeira's 'white gold' paid for this Flemish portrait of St Peter

🍴 Pavement café (£) in Praça do Município

♿ Few

✋ Moderate

↔ Museu 'A Cidade do Açúcar' (➤ 38)

works by known artists, scholars have now deduced that they are principally the work of leading painters based in Bruges and Antwerp in the late 15th and early 16th centuries, including Gerard David (1468–1523), Dieric Bouts (died 1475) and Jan Provost (1465–1529). Several paintings include portraits of the donors, wealthy merchants who made a fortune from the Madeiran sugar trade. One fine example shows an Italian merchant, Simon Acciaiuoli, kneeling at prayer with his Scottish wife, Mary Drummond, in a painting of the Descent from the Cross, while another shows Simon Gonçalves da Câmara, the grandson of Zarco, Madeira's discoverer, and his family.

7

Pico do Arieiro

Drive to the top of Madeira's third highest peak for raw volcanic landscapes and spectacular views, best enjoyed at sunset or sunrise.

Pico do Arieiro (1,818m) is the third highest peak on Madeira. It is easily reached from central Funchal by driving north on the EN 103 road to the Poiso Pass, and then taking the EN 202 west.

As you climb, the green woodland that cloaks much of central Madeira gives way to a wilder upland landscape of sheep grazed turf. The sense of travelling to a different world is reinforced by the cloud belt, which hangs at around 1,200m. Passing through this miasma of swirling mist and driving rain, you will emerge in brilliant sunshine. Bare rock soon becomes the predominant feature in the landscape, and only the hardiest of plants can find any toehold among the clinker-like tufa that makes up the summit of Pico do Arieiro.

To compensate for the lack of vegetation, there are tremendous views over an endless succession of knife-edge ridges and sheer cliffs. Cotton-wool clouds hang in the valleys far below and the only sound comes from the wind. The predominant colours are purple, burnt orange and chocolate brown, a reminder of Madeira's volcanic origins. The rocks are even more vividly colourful when lit by the red and orange rays of the setting sun, or the pink light of dawn.

🚶 81C3

🍴 Restaurant (££) and snack bar (£) in the Pousada do Pico do Arieiro Hotel on the summit

❓ You can stay at Pousada do Pico do Arieiro (➤ 104), an 18-room government-run hotel at the summit (☎ 230 110)

Energetic walkers can follow the footpath that links Pico do Arieiro to Madeira's highest peak, Pico Ruivo

8

Quinta do Palheiro Ferreiro

Tropical meets temperate in Madeira's finest garden

The botanical riches of Africa, Asia and the Americas are combined in the beautifully landscaped gardens of this aristocratic estate.

Of all the gardens on Madeira, those surrounding the Quinta do Palheiro Ferreiro (also known as Blandy's Gardens) are the most rewarding. Here the spirit of the English garden has been transposed to Madeira, where full advantage has been taken of the frost-free environment. Plants that would curl up and die further north, or which have to be cosseted in the hothouse, thrive here out of doors. To create this lovely garden, successive generations of the Blandy family have been able to draw on the limitless treasures of the botanical world, planting gorgeous proteas from southern Africa, flame-flowered climbers from southern America, sweetly scented Japanese flowering shrubs, and Chinese trees with exotically patterned bark. The result is a garden full of surprises and unexpected plant combinations.

The English influence is evident in the division of the garden into a series of 'rooms' divided by hedges and linked by mixed borders. Smaller intimate areas, such as the peaceful and shady Ladies' Garden, with its topiary peacocks, give way to more open areas, such as the sweeping lawns surrounding the baroque chapel built by the Count of Carvalhal. The wealthy count was the original owner of this aristocratic estate, which the Blandy family acquired in 1885. Part of the estate remains exactly as the count laid it out in the late 18th century, including the stately avenue of gnarled old plane trees that leads up to his original mansion. Beyond the mansion is an extensive area of informal woodland, signposted 'Inferno' (Hell), where blue morning glory vines trail among primeval tree ferns from New Zealand.

✛ 61D1

✉ Palheiro Ferreiro, 8km east of Funchal

☎ 793 044

🕐 Mon–Fri 9:30–12:30. Closed Sat, Sun, 1 Jan, Easter, 1 May, 25 Dec

🚌 Town bus 37

♿ Few

✋ Moderate

9
Sé (Funchal Cathedral)

Founded in 1485, Funchal's cathedral is one of Madeira's oldest buildings and a link with the island's original settlers.

Portugal's King Manuel I was so proud of his newly acquired island province that, in 1485, he decided to send one of Lisbon's top architects, Pedro Enes, to build a new cathedral for Funchal. The result, completed in 1514, is essentially a sombre building, although it is enlivened with Arabic-style architectural details. The most lavish exterior decoration is found not around the entrance portal, as is customary, but at the east end of the church, where the roofline is decorated with pinnacles shaped like miniature minarets. These echo the shape of the spire, which is covered in glazed *azulejos* (tiles) that were originally intended to protect the structure from wind and rain, rather than act as decoration. The comparatively plain portal bears King Manuel I's coat of arms at the top, incorporating the red cross of the Knights Templar, of which Manuel was the Grand Master.

The cool interior of the cathedral reveals its secrets only slowly as your eyes adapt to the darkness. High above the nave is a carved wooden ceiling inlaid with geometric designs in ivory. If you look long enough, or use binoculars, you will begin to make out strange animals and exotic flowers among the designs. Easier to appreciate are the choir stalls, boldly carved with near-lifesize figures of the Apostles, painted in gold against a background of powder blue. The Apostles are dressed in stylish hats, cloaks, tunics, boots and belts, giving us a good idea of the kind of clothes worn by prosperous Madeiran sugar merchants when the stalls were carved in the early 16th century. More entertaining scenes from contemporary life are to be found carved on the undersides of the choir seats. As well as cherubs, you will find monkeys and pigs and a porter carrying a pigskin full of wine.

✝ 22B2

✉ Largo da Sé

☎ 228 155

🕐 Daily 9–12:30, 4–5:30 (with services early morning and early evening)

🍴 Many pavement cafes (£) on the cathedral square

♿ Few

✋ Free

↔ Museu de Arte Sacra (► 22)

Playfully inventive pinnacles and an azulejos-covered spire on Funchal's cathedral

10
Zona Velha
(Old Town), Funchal

For atmosphere, inexpensive food and authentic Portuguese fado *music, Funchal's Zona Velha is the best place to head.*

✚ 33D2

✉ Located in the eastern part of the city

🍽 Some of the city's best restaurants are here (£–££)

↔ Mercado dos Lavradores (➤ 20), Fortaleza de São Tiago (➤ 34)

Funchal's Zona Velha (Old Town), formerly the city's slum, is now an area of quaint cobbled streets with craft shops occupying the low, one-roomed houses where at one time whole families slept, ate and played. The former boatyard has been filled in to create the base station for the Teleféricos da Madeiras (Madeira Cable Car, ➤ 111). At the eastern end, under the walls of the Fortaleza de São Tiago (➤ 34), there is a tiny black-pebble beach (the Praia da Barreirinha) where local people still come to bathe and eat grilled sardines sold by street vendors. The Old Town's last remaining fishermen also repair their boats here.

The beach remains popular despite the new lido, complete with swimming pools and sea-bathing facilities, just beyond the fortress. Opposite the lido stands the Igreja do Socorro (also called Santa Maria Maior), rebuilt several times since it was founded in the 16th century in thanksgiving for the ending of an epidemic. By contrast, the tiny Capela do Corpo Santo, in the heart of the old town, remains a simple 16th-century fishermen's chapel.

Surrounding the chapel are the numerous pavement cafés and restaurants that make the Zona Velha the bustling heart of Funchal's nightlife. Many restaurants specialise in fresh fish, and it is to here that Portuguese holiday-makers come for *bacalhau* (salt cod) or *arroz de mariscos* (seafood risotto). Several restaurants also offer *fado* music, that strangely plaintive and addictive import from the back streets of Lisbon in which the singer bemoans his or her star-crossed fate.

Funchal's Old Town is now an interesting mix of low houses, workshops and restaurants

What to See

Above: *herbal carpets at the Botanical Garden (Jardim Botânico)* Right: *azulejos depicting Madeira's grape harvest*

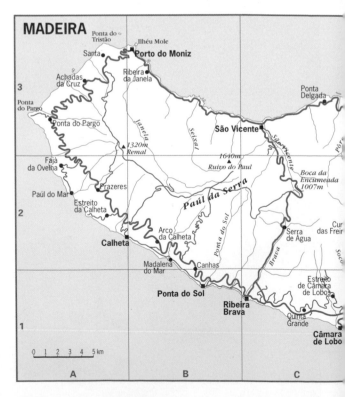

MADEIRA

Ponta do Tristão

Ilhéu Mole

Porto do Moniz

Santa

Achadas da Cruz

Ribeira da Janela

Ponta Delgada

3

Ponta do Pargo

Ponta do Pargo

Janela

Seixal

São Vicente

▲ 1320m Remal

S.Vicente

Fajã da Ovelha

1640m *Ruivo do Paul*

Pôrto

Boca da Encumeada 1007m

Paúl do Mar

Prazeres

2

Estreito da Calheta

Paúl da Serra

Arco da Calheta

Ponta do Sol

Serra de Água

Cur das Freir

Calheta

Madalena do Mar

Canhas

Brava

Soca

Ponta do Sol

Estreito de Câmara de Lobos

Ribeira Brava

Quinta Grande

1

0 1 2 3 4 5 km

Câmara de Lobo

A | **B** | **C**

Masts fill Funchal's yachting marina

PORTO SANTO

Ponta do Varadouro

Ilhéu de Ferro

Camacha
Lapeiras
Ilhéu das Cenouras
Serra de Dentro

Pico de 283m
Ana Ferreira
Ponta
Pedras Pretas
Vila Baleira (Porto Santo)

Ilhéu de Baixo

Ilhéu de Cima

0   5 km

Arco de São Jorge

Ponta de São Jorge

São Jorge

Santana

Ponta de Clérigo

Faial

Porto da Cruz

Ponta do Espigão Amarelo

Grande de São Jorge

1862m
co Ruivo

1818m
Pico de Arieiro

Ribeiro Frio

São Roque do Faial

Amamho

Machico

Ponta de São Lourenço

Ponta do Castela

Ilhéu de Agostinho

Ponta das Gaivotas

Ilhéu de Fora

Santa Luzia

Poiso
2400m

Santo António da Serra

Boaventura

Machico

38?m
Pico dos
Barcelos

Monte

Camacha

Santa Cruz

ILHAS DESERTAS

Ilhéu Chão

479m

Deserta Grande

São Gonçalo

Caniço

Ponta do Taboqueir

São Martinho

Funchal

Garajau

Caniço de Baixa
Ponta da Oliveira

383m

Bugio

Ponta da Cruz

0   5 km

D   E   F

Funchal

Far from being the provincial island backwater you might expect from its remote location, Madeira's capital is a bustling city of 100,000 people (a third of the island's population). Visitors from mainland Portugal frequently refer to Funchal as 'little Lisbon' because of its elegant architecture, fashionable shops and lively cafés. Again like Lisbon, the city streets twist and tumble up and down the steep hillside that rises from the harbour. Only in the city centre are the streets level, and here the main avenues and squares are elegantly paved with black and white stone forming mosaic-work patterns based on heraldic flowers or arabesques. Flowering trees provide shade from the sun, while the heady scent of jasmine betrays the presence of one of Funchal's many hidden patios and courtyard gardens.

> *'The best houses have a
> balcony painted green;
> these balconies present a
> gay sight in the afternoon,
> being full of ladies, who
> converse with their
> neighbours across the street.'*
>
> ISABELLA DE FRANÇA
> *Journal of a visit to Madeira
> and Portugal*
> (1853–4)

Funchal

Funchal means 'fennel' and the city's name is said to derive from the abundance of fennel plants that Zarco, the island's discoverer, found growing here when he arrived in 1420. Zarco chose this spot to found the future capital because of its sheltered natural harbour, which today is filled with every kind of vessel, from rusty container ships to luxurious cruise liners.

High above the harbour, on the cliff tops west of the city, is the Hotel Zone, where most visitors to Madeira stay. The area is almost a self-contained town, with its tourist shops and supermarkets, its cinemas and restaurants. The city is divided into three sectors by its rivers, now enclosed between high embankments to prevent the flash floods that previously claimed several lives.

In the eastern sector of the city is the Zona Velha, or Old Town (► 26), with its many restaurants. The central sector contains a jumble of embroidery factories, crumbling town houses and shops selling pungent salt cod and dried herbs. Most of Funchal's cultural sights are packed into the maze of streets in the westernmost third of the city, focused around two of Madeira's oldest buildings, the Sé (► 25) and the Alfândega Velha (Old Customs House), now the Madeiran parliament building.

Above: a bird's eye view of Funchal's fine natural harbour

What to See in Funchal

ADEGAS DE SÃO FRANCISCO (► 16, TOP TEN)

CONVENTO DE SANTA CLARA

High walls surround the Convent of the Poor Clares, shutting off from the world one of Madeira's oldest religious foundations. Santa Clara was founded in 1496 by João Gonçalves de Câmara, one of the grandsons of Zarco, the discoverer of Madeira. Zarco's granddaughter, Dona Isabella, was installed as the first abbess, establishing a tradition of aristocratic patronage that ensured that the convent was richly endowed. Many a daughter of wealthy parents was forced to take the veil on reaching her eighteenth birthday, a practice that was supposed to confer spiritual benefits on both parents and child. The convent became a popular tourist attraction in the 19th century, when visitors would come ostensibly to buy flowers made of feathers and sample sweetmeats made by the nuns, but in reality hoping to catch sight of some

---

🔢 32A3
✉ Calçada de Santa Clara
☎ 742 602
🕐 Daily 9–12, 3–6; ring for entry if door is closed, but not over the lunch period
♿ Few
💲 Free
↔ Museu Freitas (► 40), Museu Municipal (► 41)

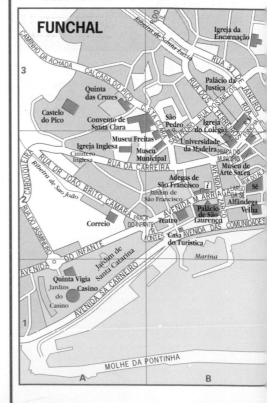

legendary beauty, tragically cut off from the delights of the world.

Today the nuns run a well-regarded kindergarten and primary school. Ring the bell on the gate and you can take a guided tour of the chapels that lie off the peaceful 15th-century cloisters. The chapels shelter an astonishing wealth of paintings, sculpture and *azulejos* tiles. The church alongside was largely rebuilt in the 17th century but it stands on the site of a 15th-century chapel where the island's first three governors, including Zarco, were buried. Glazed *azulejos* decorate the domed church tower, and there are more ancient tiles, faded but still impressive, covering the walls. Above is a typical Madeiran church ceiling of timber, painted with floral patterns and a galleon in full sail.

Above: *The cloisters of the Poor Clares*
Below: *Moorish influences in architecture*

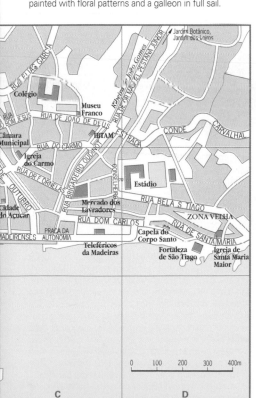

+ 33D2
+ Rua do Portão de São Tiago
+ 226 456
+ Mon–Sat 10–12:30, 2–5:30. Closed Sun, public hols
+ Restaurants and cafés (£–££) nearby in the Zona Velha
+ Few
+ Moderate
+ Zona Velha (➤ 26)

The 17th-century fortress of St James now houses an art gallery

FORTALEZA DE SÃO TIAGO ✪

Attracted by stories of Madeira's massive sugar-derived wealth, French, English, Algerian and Turkish pirates regularly attacked Funchal from the 16th century, looting churches and wine cellars and killing anyone who stood in their way. In response, Madeira's governor ordered the construction of massive walls and fortifications, which were extended and reinforced over a 100-year period. Built in 1614, the Fortress of St James was one of the last fortifications to be completed. It is also the only fort fully open to the public, since the others are still used by the Portuguese military. Newly restored, the building now houses a museum of contemporary art, but the rather unexciting works on display are a distraction from the real interest of the fortress – the maze of passages, staircases and towers, which make a perfect playground for children, and the views over the rooftops of Funchal to be had from the ramparts.

+ 33C3
+ Rua do Visconde de Anadia 44
+ 223 141
+ Mon–Fri 10–12:30, 2:30–5:30. Closed Sat, Sun, public hols
+ Few
+ Moderate
+ Museu Franco (➤ 40)

IBTAM HANDICRAFTS INSTITUTE ✪✪

IBTAM is the body that oversees standards in Madeira's economically important embroidery industry, and the small museum on the first floor of its headquarters building is a showcase for Madeiran handicrafts. The rather drab and old-fashioned displays are brought to life by the vibrant colours of traditional island costume, including scarlet and yellow skirts, waistcoats and scarves. Also on display are intricately embroidered tablecloths and bedspreads, and diaphanous nightgowns. Displayed on the staircase leading up to the museum is an impressive tapestry depicting a flower-filled Madeiran landscape, made in 1958–61 and comprising some 7 million stitches.

JARDIM BOTÂNICO ✪✪✪

Nineteenth-century writers bestowed many fanciful names on Madeira to describe the island's botanical wealth – 'a floating greenhouse' and 'God's botanical garden' being among them. The first plant seeds were probably carried by oceanic currents from West Africa, or reached Madeira in bird droppings. Thriving in the island's fertile volcanic soil, species evolved that are unique to the island. Early settlers may have destroyed many more plants as they slashed and burned the island's dense vegetation. Zarco ordered the island's woods to be set alight, and such was the ferocity of the resulting blaze that the explorers were driven back to their ships, eventually being forced to put out to sea to escape the heat.

Even so, it is unlikely that the whole island was burned, for several large areas of wilderness remain on Madeira, and the Botanical Garden displays examples of the kind of trees and shrubs that make up Madeira's virgin forest. Among them is the aptly named dragon tree, with its smooth bark and claw-like leaf clusters, valued since ancient times for its red sap used for cloth dyeing.

Competing with the dragon tree are the many strange and colourful plants introduced to Madeira from far-distant lands, all displayed here in a series of terraced beds. Stars of the show include the tropical orchids (in flower from November to March), while other beds are devoted to the plants that underpin Madeira's cut-flower trade – such as bird of paradise plants and arum lilies – and a fine collection of cacti and sculptural agaves.

✚ 61D1
✉ Quinta do Bom Sucesso, Caminho do Meio
☎ 211 200
🕐 Daily 8–6. Closed 25 Dec
🍴 Café (£) in grounds
🚌 Town bus 31
♿ Few
✋ Moderate (includes entrance to nearby Jardim dos Loiros ➤ 36)

Carpet bedding in the Botanical Garden

➕ 61D1
✉ Caminho do Meio
☎ 211 200
🕐 Daily 9–6. Closed 25, 31 Dec
🚌 Town bus 31
♿ Few
🏛 Moderate (includes entrance to nearby Jardim Botânico ➤ 35)

JARDIM DOS LOIROS ⭐

Exotic screeches, whoops and squawks advertise the presence of this tropical bird garden, where even the brightest flowers are put in the shade by the plumage of cockatoos, parrots, parakeets and macaws. Children will enjoy the antics of the birds, which are displayed in aviaries dotted around the gardens.

➕ 32A1
✉ Avenida do Infante
🕐 24 hours
🍴 Café (£) in grounds
♿ Few
🏛 Free
↔ Adegas de São Francisco (➤ 16)

JARDIM DE SANTA CATARINA ⭐

This public park is named after the Chapel of St Catherine, founded in 1425 by Constança Rodriguez, wife of Zarco. The little chapel, with its attractive porch and holy water stoup, stands on a terrace from which there are good views of the harbour. Elsewhere the park is dotted with sculptures, ranging from a modernist fountain featuring a female torso to the vigorous bronze figure of the *Semeador*, the Sower (1919), by Francisco Franco (➤ 40). The Sower metaphorically broadcasts his seed across immaculate flower beds, and the upper part of the garden, with its aviaries and children's playground, has many fine tropical flowering trees. From the park, you can walk uphill into the well-tended and shady grounds of the Quinta Vigia, the pink-painted mansion that forms the official residence of Madeira's president. On the opposite side of the road is the Hospicio da Princesa, built as a tuberculosis sanatorium in 1859, with another fine garden featuring several ancient dragon trees.

Above: *a denizen of the Tropical Bird Garden – a scarlet macaw*
Below: *'The Sower' symbolically scatters seeds in the Jardim de Santa Catarina*

Around the Harbour

Early evening is a good time to do this walk, ending up with a view from a pavement café of Madeira's brief sunset.

Start at the tourist office in Avenida Arriaga and turn right.

Funchal's residents gather to chat in the tree-shaded Jardim de São Francisco, to the right of the Adegas de São Francisco wine lodge (► 16). Opposite is the remarkable 1920s Toyota showroom, decorated with tile pictures of the Monte toboggan (► 21). Next door is the Municipal Theatre of 1888 (you can go and look inside if there is no performance) and the trendy theatre bar, with its own tree-shaded patio, alongside.

Turn left beside the theatre, down Rua do Conselheiro José Silvestre Ribeiro.

At the bottom, on the left, is the Casa do Turista (► 108), an elegantly furnished town house packed with quality products from Madeira and mainland Portugal.

A panel of 1920s azulejos adorns the Toyota showroom on Avenida Arriaga

Turn right, if you wish, to walk through the busy port and out along the Molhe da Pontinha, the great sea wall that encloses the harbour. Alternatively, cross to the sea wall side of Avenida do Mar and turn left.

The 16th-century Palácio de São Lourenço on your left (► 38) bristles with ancient cannon. To your right is the yacht marina, enclosed by a high sea wall painted by visiting sailors with pictures recording their visit. Seafood restaurants line the landward side, while ice-cream booths and floating restaurants lie further up along Avenida do Mar. Beyond, on the left, is the Madeiran Regional Parliament, with its circular modern debating chamber.

Turn left up the street just before this building to reach the cathedral square (► 25), with its many pavement cafés.

Distance
1.5km

Time
1 hour

Start point
Tourist Information Centre, Avenida Arriaga 16
✚ 32B2

End point
Largo da Sé
✚ 32B2

Lunch
Marina Terrace (££)
✉ Marina do Funchal
☎ 230 547

37

MERCADO DOS LAVRADORES (► 20, TOP TEN)

MUSEU 'A CIDADE DO AÇÚCAR'

This new museum is constructed around the excavated remains of a house built in 1495 for Jeanin Esmerandt, a Flemish merchant working for the Bruges-based Company Despars. The significance of the house is that Christopher Columbus twice stayed here as a guest of Esmerandt: once in 1480, and again in 1498 (after his pioneering voyage across the Atlantic to the Americas) when he stayed for six days. The original house was demolished in 1876 and excavated in 1989. Finds from the excavation exhibited here include pottery, food remains (nuts, seashells and animal bones), jewellery, coins and bone buttons. Also on display here are ceramic sugar cones, similar to those which feature on Funchal's coat of arms, and 16th-century engravings of the sugar-making process. The enormous wealth that sugar brought to Funchal is represented here by religious paintings and statues acquired by the city's merchants.

MUSEU DE ARTE SACRA (► 22, TOP TEN)

MUSEU FORTALEZA

Housed within the bastions of the Palácio de São Lourenço (Palace of St Lawrence), the Fortress Museum is only open to those who ring in advance and book a place on the guided tour. If you don't want to do this, you can at least look at the fortress's 16th-century carved stone gateway, tucked away off Avenida Arriaga, opposite the tourist office. The fortress was still incomplete in 1566 when Bertrand de Montluc, the French pirate, raided Madeira, rounded up 250 of the most prominent citizens and put them to the sword within the fortress walls. Now it is classified as a national monument and is one of Portugal's best-preserved early fortifications. Tours take in the grand rooms installed when the fortress was converted to a palace for the military and civilian governors of Madeira in the 19th century. Also on display are historic weapons.

+ 32C2
⊠ Praça do Colombo
☎ 236 910
⊙ Tue–Fri 9–12:30, 2–5:30. Closed Sat, Sun, Mon, public hols
Ⅱ Cafés (£) in nearby Largo da Sé (cathedral square)
♿ Few
Moderate
↔ Museu de Arte Sacra (► 22)

Above: the elegant inner courtyard of Funchal's Town Hall

+ 32B2
⊠ Praça do Colombo
☎ 202 530
⊙ Wed, Fri, by guided tour at 10:30 and 3
Ⅱ Cafés (£) in nearby Largo da Sé (cathedral square)
♿ Few
Moderate
↔ Museu de Arte Sacra (► 22)

Exploring Funchal's Architecture

Discover Funchal's rich architectural heritage on a stroll through the city centre

Start at the Câmara Municipal ('Town Hall')

A symphony in monochrome. basalt and marble in Praça do Município

The elegant 18th-century mansion was built for the wealthy Count of Carvalhal but sold by his profligate heirs. The delightful palm-filled courtyard features a graceful sculpture of *Leda and the Swan* (1880). Turn your back on the entrance to view Praça do Município (Town Square), paved with grey basalt and white marble in a fish-scale pattern. To the right, gesticulating saints decorate the façade of the Igreja di Colégio, the Jesuit church, founded in 1574. To the left is the Bishop's Palace of 1600, now housing the Museu de Arte Sacra (Sacred Art Museum ➤ 22).

Cross the square, heading for the far right-hand corner. Walk up shop-lined Rua C Pestana and carry straight on at the next junction, along Rua da Carreira.

Three doors up on the left, in Rua da Carreira, is the entrance to the Pátio complex, with its bookshops and courtyard café. Try coffee here, or buy typical Madeiran *bolo de mel* (literally 'honey cake' but actually made with molasses) at the baker's further up on the left.

Walk up Rua da Carreira.

As you dip in and out of the street's characterful shops, look up to see the pretty wrought-iron balconies that decorate many of the upper storeys. Among the best houses is No 155.

The third turn right (Rua do Quebra Costas) leads to the English Church (completed 1822), set in a pretty garden.

At the end of Rua da Carreira is the British Cemetery (Cimitero Inglesa), the burial ground of Madeira's Protestants of all nationalities, worth visiting for its many poignant 19th-century memorials and epitaphs.

Distance
1km

Time
30 minutes

Start point
Câmara Municipal (Town Hall), Praça do Município
 32B2

End point
British Cemetery, Rua da Carreira. To enter the cemetery, ring the bell at No. 235
32A2

Lunch
O Pátio Café
Rua da Carreira 43
227 376

MUSEU FRANCO

This quiet and little-visited museum celebrates the artistic achievements of two brothers born on Madeira but who achieved fame on the wider European stage. Henrique Franco (1883–1961) was a painter and his older brother Francisco (1855–1955) was a sculptor. Both studied in Paris, where they were friendly with Picasso, Degas and Modigliani, but their careers were largely centred on the Portuguese capital, Lisbon.

The first part of the museum is devoted to a series of Gauginesque portraits, painted by Henrique. He often painted his subjects – from weather-beaten peasants to industrialists and aristocrats – against a colourful background of flowers and foliage reminiscent of the Madeiran landscape.

Francisco's vigorous but monochrome sculptures in the second part of the museum are evidence of a busy life devoted to designing public memorials, coins, medals and postage stamps, including such sculptures as the Zarco monument in central Funchal (➤ 45) and the *Semeador* in the Jardim de Santa Catarina (➤ 36).

MUSEU FREITAS

Halfway up the steep and cobbled Calçada de Santa Clara is this balconied town house, whose stately rooms provide a glimpse of life on Madeira at any time over the last 150 years.

The first part of the museum consists of a newly built gallery covering the history of *azulejos* tiles, those brightly coloured ceramics that decorate church walls all over Madeira, as well as domestic homes. Originating in the Islamic east, the practice of using tiles spread from Persia to Portugal via Moorish North Africa and Spain. The island of Madeira lacked suitable clays to produce its own tiles and so imported them from Seville in the 16th century, and later from the Netherlands. Examples of tiles from Santa Clara convent are among the earliest exhibits, while the last flowering of tile manufacture includes some lovely art-nouveau designs.

The second part of the museum consists of the house bequeathed to Funchal by the lawyer Dr Frederico de Freitas, in 1978. The rambling mansion dates back to the late 17th century, when it was built by the Count of Calçada. Art-nouveau furnishings, a pretty conservatory in the garden and a glass-roofed winter garden all lend charm to a house crammed with fascinating objects collected by Dr Freitas during the course of his travels around the world – including over 2,000 jugs. The collections include oriental carpets, religious paintings, *azulejos* and fine antique furnishings, as well as 17th- and 18th-century hand-carved and painted crib figures originating from mainland Portugal and the Portuguese colonies of Goa and Macau.

Opposite top: the intimate Winter Garden, with its cane furniture and art-nouveau doors, in Museu Freitas

MUSEU MUNICIPAL ⭐⭐

The Municipal Museum is one of the few on Madeira that children genuinely enjoy, thanks to the aquarium on the ground floor. This is stocked with the fish that are typically caught off Madeiran shores, including morose-looking grouper fish, hungry-eyed moray eels and bottom-dwelling flounders. Upstairs, there is an extensive collection of stuffed birds and animals, including sharks with gaping jaws and giant crabs with metre-long claws. Displays of typical Madeiran birds are as close as you are likely to get to the more elusive species that like to nest on inaccessible cliffs.

➕ 32B2
✉ Rua da Mouraria 31
☎ 229 761
🕐 Tue–Fri 10–6, Sat, Sun, public hols 12–6. Closed 25 Dec, 1 Jan
♿ Few
🍴 Moderate
↔ Convento de Santa Clara (► 32), Museu Freitas (► 40)

Jaws meets Municipal Museum

Food & Drink

Madeiran cooking is deliciously simple: fish and meat grilled over a charcoal fire and flavoured with garlic and herbs. Eaten with warm bread, straight from the oven, this is food to be savoured in the flower-scented air of a balmy Madeiran evening.

On the Rocks
A good Madeiran any-time-of-day-snack is *lapas* – grilled limpets served in the shell, each in a puddle of garlic butter which you soak up with plenty of spongy home-made bread: in taste and texture, limpets are very like snails.

Madeira's specialities are *espada* and *espetada*, two totally different dishes with confusingly similar names. Fish-lovers should opt for *espada*, the grilled or fried meat of the scabbard fish, ugly black-skinned creatures with large eyes and razor-sharp teeth that are sold in every Madeiran fish market. The tasty bone-free fish with firm white flesh is usually marinated in lemon juice or vinegar before cooking, and may be served with split grilled bananas. Upmarket restaurants also *flambé* the fish in Madeira wine and add imported seafood, such as shrimps and mussels, to the sauce.

Fish is an everyday dish on Madeira. On special occasions, Madeirans eat kebabs – called *espetada* – made from cubes of prime beef, rubbed in sea salt and minced garlic and skewered on a fresh bay twig. To enjoy this dish at its most authentic, you have to eat it at a village festival, or find a restaurant that grills the meat over a wood fire for extra fragrance. Beef features again in the popular lunchtime staple of *prego no prato*, a sandwich made from robust country bread liberally spread with garlic butter and enclosing a tender chunk of grilled steak.

Seafood and Soups

Many restaurants on Madeira specialise in seafood, though most is imported and a seafood

From top: *charcoal-grilled* espetada *(beef),* garlic-soused limpets *and* scabbard fish *(espada)*

42

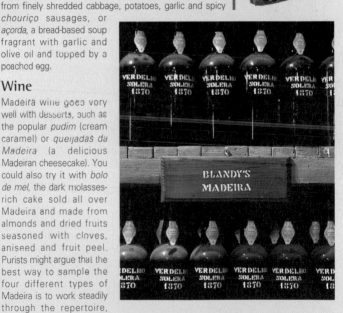

platter can be expensive. Fish soup (*caldeirada*) is, by contrast, delicious and cheap, being based on stock made from the heads and bones of locally caught fish, such as sea-bream, black-tail, barracuda and tuna. Also popular is *arroz de marisco* – seafood rice – made from saffron rice, squid, prawns and clams. Soups, influenced by mainland Portuguese cuisine, are substantial dishes – more hearty casserole than appetiser. Try *caldo verde*, made from finely shredded cabbage, potatoes, garlic and spicy *chouriço* sausages, or *açorda*, a bread-based soup fragrant with garlic and olive oil and topped by a poached egg.

Wine

Madeira wine goes very well with desserts, such as the popular *pudim* (cream caramel) or *queijadas da Madeira* (a delicious Madeiran cheesecake). You could also try it with *bolo de mel*, the dark molasses-rich cake sold all over Madeira and made from almonds and dried fruits seasoned with cloves, aniseed and fruit peel. Purists might argue that the best way to sample the four different types of Madeira is to work steadily through the repertoire, starting with dry *sercial* as an aperitif or accompaniment to fish, then moving on to medium-dry *verdelho* with the main course, and nutty *bual* with dessert, reserving the rich, dark *malmsey* to drink with coffee.

Few Madeirans would drink fortified Madeiran wine with their food, preferring something lighter, such as semi-sparkling *vinho verde*, imported from mainland Portugal, or locally produced red and white wines, which are drunk young and fruity. Also popular as a pick-me-up is *poncha*, a cocktail of sugar-cane spirit, called *aguardente*, mixed with honey and fresh lemon juice.

Good companions – bolo de mel *(honey cake) and vintage Madeira*

Other Drinks

Coral beer is an excellent light lager-style beer, brewed on the island. A popular summer wine is *vinho verde* – green wine – named not for its colour (straw yellow) but for its youthfulness.

☩ 32B2
✉ Rua da Carreira 43
🕐 Daily 9–6
↔ Museu Municipal (➤ 41)

The graceful Pátio café makes a good coffee stop

O PÁTIO ⭐

O Pátio (The Patio) is a charming building dating from the 1860s, consisting of a courtyard and café, open to the sky, shaded by palms and surrounded by an arcade of small shops. Rising from the cobbled courtyard is a charming double staircase with wrought-iron balustrades, leading up to a fanciful balcony of similar design, looking just like a saloon bar in some Wild West movie.

The upper storey houses the photographic studio of Vicente Gomes da Silva, founded in 1865, when the art of photography was still relatively new. In fact, this was the first commercial photographic studio to be established in the whole of Portugal; such was the demand for holiday souvenirs from wealthy visitors to Madeira that Gomes da Silva felt confident in pouring a small fortune into the purchase of mahogany and brass-bound plate cameras, together with all the paraphernalia of the darkroom. The studio was open as a museum until recently, but it has now been closed until a new home can be found for the 380,000 or so photographs that have survived in the Vicentes collection, a rich resource covering nearly 140 years of island history.

☩ 32A3
✉ Rua do Castelo
🕐 Daily 9–6
🚫 None
♿ Free
↔ Quinta das Cruzes
(➤ 45)

PICO (CASTELO DO PICO)

It is a sweaty, heart-pounding climb up to the Pico, or Radio Peak as it is known locally because of the naval communications masts bristling from its heights. It is worth the effort for the *castelo*, built in 1632–40 to warn off sea attack. A walk around the walls is rewarding for the views down across Funchal's rooftops and up to the wooded heights above the city. A small exhibition room in the castle traces its history through old engravings.

QUINTA DAS CRUZES ✪✪✪

Of the many fine mansions built by wealthy merchants around Funchal, the Quinta das Cruzes (the Mansion of the Crosses) is the only one open to the public. Zarco, the discoverer of Madeira and the island's first governor, built his house on this site in the 1450s, but little remains from this era except for some architectural fragments displayed in the gardens. These include gravestones, crosses and broken pieces of church fonts, as well as all that remains of Funchal's pillory, where miscreants were once publicly flogged. Most striking of all are two stone window frames, carved with dancing figures and man-eating lions in the style known as Manueline, after the reigning monarch.

The present house dates from the 17th century, when it was built for the Lomelino family, wealthy wine merchants from Genova. Furnished in the Empire style that was popular at the time, the rooms are arranged thematically, with sections devoted to oriental art, French porcelain, topographical views and portraits, costume and crib figures.

The basement contains an unusual collection of furniture made from recycled packing cases. Sugar was once so precious that it was shipped in chests made from best Brazilian satinwood. Once competition from the New World destroyed Madeira's sugar trade, enterprising cabinet-makers reused the wood to make the fine cupboards displayed here.

+ 33A3
✉ Calçada do Pico 1
☎ 741 382
🕐 Tue–Sat 10–12:30, 2–5:30, Sun 10–1. Closed Mon, public hols
♿ Few
💷 Moderate
↔ Convento de Santa Clara (► 32)

Did you know ?

Ornately carved stone pillories, such as the one in the grounds of the Quinta das Cruzes, are found in the main square of most towns in Portugal. In the Middle Ages, criminals were tied to these columns and whipped. Legal proclamations were also read from here so they came to symbolise local government, becoming a focal point for meetings and community politics

SÉ (CATHEDRAL ► 25, TOP TEN)

ZONA VELHA (OLD TOWN ► 26, TOP TEN)

Above: *a Manueline-style window frame in the Quinta das Cruzes gardens*
Left: *Zarco, Madeira's discoverer, built the original Quinta das Cruzes*

JOÃO GONÇALVES ZARCO

45

Western Madeira

The western third of Madeira used to be the least accessible: just getting to Ribeira Brava, the starting point for exploring the west, took more than an hour from Funchal. However, in 1997 transport on the island was revolutionised with the opening of the Via Rápida expressway, so that Ribeira Brava is now only 15 minutes away. From here you can explore picturesque fishing villages, bleak moorland and mountains cloaked in dense forest. The south coast is one long ribbon of vineyards and banana plantations, with steep lanes linking one hamlet to the next. By contrast, the north coast road offers some of the most dramatic scenery on the island, with the boiling ocean dashing against huge black rocks and waterfalls cascading from cliff top to sea.

> *'Most of us preferred walking to being carried along this ledge cut in the cliff several hundred feet above the sea. The scenery is most splendid, with very beautiful waterfalls descending from a great height.'*

ELLEN TAYLOR
describing the north coast road in
Madeira: Its Scenery and How to See It
(1882)

———————•———————

The north coast road near Porto Moniz

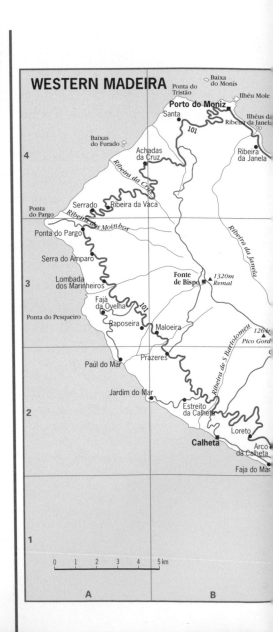

WESTERN MADEIRA

Baixa
do Monís

Ponta do
Tristão

Ilhéu Mole

Porto do Moniz

Santa

Ilhéus da
Ribeira da Janela

101

Baixas
do Furado

Achadas
da Cruz

4

Ribeira da Cruz

Ribeira
da Janela

Serrado

Ribeira da Vaca

Ponta
do Pargo

Ribeira dos Moinhos

Ribeira da Janela

Ponta do Pargo

Serra do Amparo

Fonte
de Bispo

1320m
Remal

3

Lombada
dos Marinheiros

Fajã
da Ovelha

101

Ponta do Pesqueiro

Raposeira

Maloeira

Ribeira de S. Bartolomeu

1269
Pico Gordo

Prazeres

Paúl do Mar

Jardim do Mar

Estreito
da Calheta

2

Loreto

Calheta

Arco
da Calheta

Faja do Mar

1

0   1   2   3   4   5 km

A

B

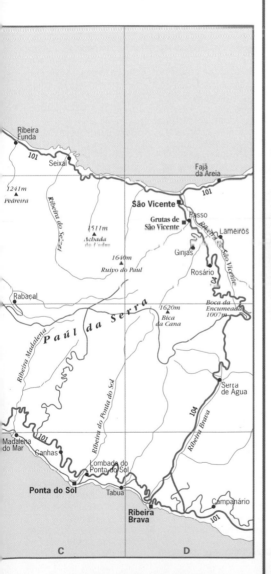

Floral carpets to celebrate Corpus Christi in the streets of Ponta do Sol

What to See in Western Madeira

BOCA DA ENCUMEADA

The Boca da Encumeada (Encumeada Pass), midway between Ribeira Brava and São Vicente, is a popular stopping-off point for round-the-island tours because of the extensive views to be had from the lookout point at the top of the pass (1,004m). Weather permitting, it is possible to see across to São Vicente on the north coast and down the Serra de Água Valley to the south coast, though more often than not you will stand in brilliant sunshine looking down on to the top of humid rain clouds.

If the weather is finer and clear, prolong your visit by following the Levada do Norte (Levada of the North) westwards: look for the sign to Folhadal opposite the café and climb up to the *levada* past the keeper's house. It is well worth exploring this path for 2km or so; you will be greeted by an abundance of wild flowers and excellent views to the south.

CALHETA 🟢

Calheta is the main town for the southwestern coast of Madeira, a fertile sunbathed region where the orange-roofed houses are lost among a sea of banana, grapevine and sugar-cane plantations. Every front garden hosts a colourful display of scarlet and pink geraniums, mauve bougainvillaea and purple passion flowers. If you come here on 7 or 8 September even the streets are covered in flowers as carpets of blooms are laid out to celebrate the Feast of Our Lady of Loreto.

Like most of the island's churches, the one in Calheta has been rebuilt many times and looks disappointingly modern. Inside, however, is a large tabernacle of ebony and silver, donated by Portugal's King Manuel I (1469–1521). The sanctuary has a fine wooden ceiling in the Moorish-influenced *mudejar* style. The sweet smell of cane syrup from the factory next door to the church may tempt you to take a tour to watch rum and molasses being produced, a vestige of an industry that was once widespread on Madeira.

If you are prepared to get lost in the maze of lanes around Calheta, it is worth seeking out two more churches. At Loreto (2km east of Calheta), the church, built by one of

---

49D2

✉ On EN 104 road, 43km northwest of Funchal

🍴 Café (£) alongside the viewpoint car park; for more substantial meals try Restaurante Encumeada (££, ☎ 952 319), on road south to Serra de Água

🚌 Bus 139

↔ Ribeira Brava (► 54)

48B2

✉ On south coast, 61km west of Funchal

🍴 Marisqueria do Camarão (££, ☎ 824 379), just east of town, on coast road to Madalena do Mar; renowned for seafood

🚌 Buses 80, 115, 139, 142

♿ None

↔ Ponta do Sol (► 52)

❓ Sugar mill (☎ 822 264) open daily during working hours, except public hols

---

Above: *Boca da Encumeada views*
Right: *blue agapanthus on the
Levada das Rabacas*

Zarco's daughters-in-law, has a
south portal carved in the lively
Manueline style typical of the early
16th century, and a *mudejar*-style
wooden ceiling.

Best of all the churches in the
area is the Capela dos Reis Magos
(Chapel of the Three Kings) at
Lombo dos Reis (between Estreito
da Calheta and Jardim do Mar,
west of Calheta). Here the chapel
houses a rare wooden reredos,
carved in Antwerp in the 16th
century with lively scenes depicting
the Adoration of the Magi.

PAÚL DA SERRA

Flat, bleak and grazed by hardy free-range cows, sheep
and goats, the Paúl da Serra comes as a surprise to
Madeiran travellers grown used to views of jagged
mountain peaks. This windswept high plateau offers
expansive views of moorland, its wild open landscape now
somewhat compromised by a forest of wind turbines, built
to supply electricity to the communities of the island's
northern coast. Even so, it is worth coming here to look for
wild bilberries in autumn and to savour the eerie
atmosphere, or to enjoy the panoramic views to be had
when the plateau is not enshrouded in cloud.

49C2
61km northwest of
Funchal, either side of
the EN 124 road
Rabaçal (► 55)

✚ 48A3
✉ 77km west of Funchal
🍴 Solar do Pargo café
(£, ☎ 882 170) in
Ponta do Pargo
🚌 Bus 142
♿ None
↔ Porto do Moniz (► 53)

PONTA DO PARGO

Visitors are drawn to the westernmost tip of Madeira by the thought that nothing now stands between them and the east coast of America except for hundreds of miles of ocean. Standing alongside the cliff-top lighthouse at Ponta do Pargo, 300m above the sea, you can try spotting fishermen who come here to catch the *pargos* (dolphin fish, no relation to the dolphin) after which Ponta do Pargo (Dolphin Point) is named. You can also pick up the Levada Calheta–Ponta do Pargo, the water channel that runs parallel to the south coast, weaving in and out of the hills as it follows the 650m contour with views south to the sea and north to the Paúl da Serra plateau. Frequent bus services pass along the nearby EN 101 road, so you can park in Ponta do Pargo, walk as far as you choose and then catch a bus back to your car.

✚ 49C1
✉ 42km west of Funchal
🍴 Beachside bar (£) in
Ponta do Sol; try also the
A Poita restaurant
(££, ☎ 974 871) in
Madalena do Mar for fish
soup and seafood
🚌 Bus 4
♿ None
↔ Ribeira Brava (► 54)

*A decorative chimney in
sunny Ponta do Sol*

PONTA DO SOL ★

Sunset is a good time to visit Ponta do Sol for uninterrupted views of fireworks in the western sky while strolling along the harbour promenade or enjoying an ice cream at the ornate seafront kiosk. Steep cobbled streets lead upwards to the church, with its unusual green ceramic font, donated by King Manuel I (1469–1521), and its ancient wooden ceilings, painted with scenes from the Life of the Virgin. Behind the church, a plaque on the wall of the Town Hall, at Rua Príncipe D Luís I, records a visit made by John dos Passos (1896–1970), the American novelist whose grandparents emigrated from this village in the mid-19th century.

The church at nearby Madalena do Mar is the burial place of an intriguing figure known as Henrique Alemão (Henry the German) – in reality King Wladyslaw III of Poland, who chose self-imposed exile on Madeira after losing the Battle of Varna in 1414. Here he became a prosperous farmer and built a chapel on the site of today's church. Tragically, Wladyslaw drowned near Cabo Girão (► 17) as his ship hit rocks on the way to Lisbon to see King Manuel I.

PORTO DO MONIZ ✪✪

Porto do Moniz is a surprisingly cosmopolitan place for a village located at the northernmost extremity of Madeira, thanks to the waterfront hotel and restaurant catering for travellers on round-the-island tours. Bones weary from walking or jolting up and down the island's roads can be revived by a good soaking in the natural rock pools in front of the hotel. These have been enlarged to create a warm sea-water bathing area, just a few feet away from the Atlantic waves that crash against Madeira's northern shore. The waves carry salt-laden spray far up into the surrounding hills, hence the ingenious use of grass and bracken fences to protect the crops growing in the fields surrounding the village. Viewed from the steep roads descending into the village, this patchwork of tiny fields and fences creates an attractive pattern.

✚ 48B4
✉ 75km northwest of Funchal
🍴 Good choice of restaurants (££), including the Cachalote (££, ☎ 853 180), specialising in seafood
🚌 Buses 80, 100
♿ None

Tiny fields (above) fenced against the spray in Porto do Moniz (below)

RIBEIRA BRAVA ⭐⭐

To understand why Ribeira Brava (Wild River) is so named, you have to visit in late autumn or winter, when the river that runs through the town centre is in full spate. For the rest of the year its harmless appearance belies its true nature. Over several thousand millennia this river has carved out a deep cleft that seems almost to divide Madeira in two, running due north from Ribeira Brava up to the Encumeada Pass and on to São Vicente, on the north coast of Madeira. The road that runs up this valley has long been an important transport route, which is why Ribeira Brava has grown into a sizeable town, with a market and a number of seafront cafés where farmers, taking their produce to Funchal, stop to break their journey.

Located just back from the seafront is the splendid Church of São Bento (St Benedict). Like most churches on Madeira it has been rebuilt many times, but there are several features remaining from the original 15th-century church, including the painted font, decorated with grapes, pomegranates and wild beasts, and the carved stone pulpit. The right-hand chapel contains a fine Flemish painting of the Nativity, surrounded by gilded woodwork.

At the north end of town, the new Museu Etnográfico da Madeira (Madeira Ethnographic Museum) offers displays on fishing, agriculture, weaving and winemaking.

➕ 49D1

✉ 32km west of Funchal

🍴 Good choice of cafés and restaurants (£–££) along the seafront road, and along the cobbled main street, Rua do Visconde

🚌 Bus 7

♿ None

↔ Boca da Encumeada (► 50)

ℹ Tourist office (☎ 951 675), in the Forte de São Bento, along the seafront road

Museu Etnográfico da Madeira

✉ Rua de São Francisco 24

☎ 952 598

🕐 Tue–Sun 10–12:30, 2–6

Terraced slopes above Ribeira Brava

Did you know ?

Madeira's native forest is called laurisilva, *in Portuguese, meaning "laurel-wood", because most of the predominant species belong to the evergreen laurel family. They include the sweetly scented bay tree, used in Madeiran cooking, and the* vinhático, *known as Madeira mahogany and used to make fine furniture.*

Along the Levada do Risco

If you are driving across the Paúl da Serra, it is well worth breaking your journey to explore this secret valley of ancient trees and mossy waterfalls.

Rabaçal is reached down a steep single track road off the Paúl da Serra plateau.

There is a car park alongside the government rest house (used by forestry workers, but with public facilities, including barbecue pits, picnic tables and toilets).

Follow the sign to the right of the car park which points down the track to the Levada do Risco.

The Levada do Risco watercourse is cut into a hillside cloaked in huge, gnarled tree heathers. The humid air has also encouraged the growth of magnificent lichens, some resembling apple-coloured seaweed, some more like hanks of grey-green hair. Local foresters use branches from the tree heather for fencing along the route.

After five minutes' walking, a path leads off to the left, signposted Levada das 25 Fontes (the Levada of the 25 Springs). Ignore this for now and carry straight on.

After another ten minutes' easy walking you will come to the Risco waterfall, pouring down from the rocky heights into a magical fern-hung bowl. To your left there are sweeping views down into the green valley of the River Janela, which this waterfall feeds.

Return the way you came. You can extend your walk by taking the slightly more difficult Levada das 25 Fontes, following the signposted path downhill and then turning right once you reach the levada. This will take you, after a 20-minute walk, to another fine waterfall with one main cascade and many smaller ones.

Distance
3km

Time
1 hour

Start/end point
Rabaçal government rest house
✚ 49C3

Lunch
No cafés in the area; take a picnic

Risco falls, the reward that awaits those who follow the lichen-hung Levada do Risco

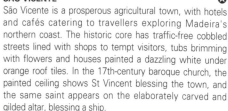

✚ 49D3

✉ 55km north of Funchal

🍽 Good choice of cafés and restaurants (£–££), including the O Virgilio restaurant (££) on the seafront (☎ 842 467)

🚌 Buses 4, 80, 132, 139

♿ None

↔ Seixal (➤ below)

Farmers take full advantage of the sun to cultivate cliff-top vineyards in Seixal, on Madeira's northwest coast

SÃO VICENTE ✪

São Vicente is a prosperous agricultural town, with hotels and cafés catering to travellers exploring Madeira's northern coast. The historic core has traffic-free cobbled streets lined with shops to tempt visitors, tubs brimming with flowers and houses painted a dazzling white under orange roof tiles. In the 17th-century baroque church, the painted ceiling shows St Vincent blessing the town, and the same saint appears on the elaborately carved and gilded altar, blessing a ship.

About 1.25km south of São Vicente, on the road to Lameiros, you will find the entrance to the Grutas de São Vicente (➤ 110).

About 2km south along the main Ribeira Brava road, a right turn leads to Ginjas and the start of a short but worthwhile walk. Carry on driving all the way through Ginjas until you meet a road junction, where you should park and walk left (uphill) towards Estanquinos. After about 30m, look for a track on the right paved with large boulders; the track passes between some drystone walls enclosing apple orchards. Climb all the way up the track (about 500m) until you meet the Levada da Fajã do Rodrigues which runs alongside a large concrete-lined reservoir on the right. Turn right to follow the *levada* for 1km through orchards and eucalyptus woods to reach a spectacular *caldeirão* (literally cauldron), watered by multiple cascades.

✚ 49C4

✉ 61km northwest of Funchal

🍽 Local wine and snacks at bar of Estalagem Brisamar guest house (££, ☎ 854 476)

🚌 Buses 80, 139

♿ None

↔ São Vicente (➤ above)

SEIXAL ✪

Seixal, midway between Porto do Moniz and São Vicente, is a good spot at which to break your journey along the north coast road (➤ 57). Here you can explore the rocky foreshore (follow the signs to Piscina for a group of big, sheltered rock pools) and walk out along the jetty for views of the coastal cliffs and waterfalls which rise up on either side of the tiny village, really little more than a hamlet. Excellent wine is produced locally from grapes grown in tiny vineyards clinging to the cliffs and protected from the wind and salt spray by fences constructed from dried bracken and tree heather. Grapes grown here are used in the driest of the four main types of Madeira wine.

Along the North Coast

The corniche that runs between Porto do Moniz (▶ 53) and São Vicente is one of Europe's most spectacular roads, built on a narrow shelf cut into the cliff face high above the raging sea.

If you drive along the road in an easterly direction, from Porto do Moniz to São Vicente, you will enjoy far-reaching views along the northern coast of Madeira. Ideally, travel the route in mid to late afternoon, when the sun is behind you and its dying embers will add their own magic to the view.

> ### Did you know ?
>
> *Built before the age of machine tools, Madeira's 19km north coast road is a major engineering achievement which took 16 years to complete. Like the island's levadas and hillside terraces, the road was created by hacking away the bare volcanic rock by hand to create the many tunnels it passes through along its narrow, winding course.*

Whichever way you choose to drive this road – east to west or west to east – you will need to travel slowly, not only to take in the spectacular coastal views, but also to avoid accidents. The road is only one vehicle wide for much of its length, so keep an eye open for approaching cars and buses, and be prepared to pull into a passing place well in advance (and remember that when Madeiran drivers flash their lights, it means 'I am coming through', not 'I am giving way to you'). At several points, waterfalls will come cascading down on top of your car – frightening as the noise can be, Madeirans look on the positive side: 'It's a free car wash', they say.

Distance
18km

Time
45 minutes

Start point
Porto do Moniz
✛ 48B4

End point
São Vicente
✛ 49D3

Lunch
O Virgílio (££)
✉ On the seafront at São Vicente
☎ 842 467

São Vicente, start point of the north coast road

Central Madeira

Central Madeira combines both the suburban sprawl of Funchal and the cinder-strewn volcanic landscape of the island's central mountain range. Though they are only 30 minutes' drive apart, one is rarely visible from the other since more often than not cloud obscures the mountain peaks. The mountains are easy enough to reach, thanks to the road that goes to the top of Pico do Arieiro, Madeira's third highest peak. Once there, paths invite exploration of the endless series of knife-edge ridges that extend to the horizon in every direction. Beyond the central mountain range, the north side of the island is dotted with tiny hamlets surrounded by a patchwork of terraced fields and orchards, plantations producing willow for basket-making, and thatched cow byres.

> *'The utter silence and absence of all habitations or cultivation gives one the sensation in these mountain solitudes of being a thousand leagues away from the haunts of men.'*
>
> ELLEN TAYLOR
> *Madeira: Its Scenery and How to See It* (1882)

On the rim of the world – the views from Pico do Arieiro

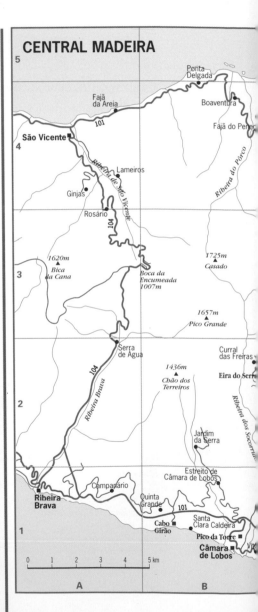

CENTRAL MADEIRA

Ponta Delgada

Fajã da Areia

Boaventura

101

Fajã do Penec

São Vicente

Lameiros

Ribeira do Pôrco

Ribeira de São Vicente

Ginjas

Rosário

104

1725m ▲ *Casado*

1620m ▲ *Bica da Cana*

Boca da Encumeada *1007m*

1657m ▲ *Pico Grande*

Serra de Água

Curral das Freiras

Eira do Serr

1436m ▲ *Cbão dos Terreiros*

104

Ribeira Brava

Ribeira dos Socorri

Jardim da Serra

Estreito de Câmara de Lobos

Campanário

Quinta Grande

Ribeira Brava

101

Cabo Girão ■

Santa Clara Caldeira

Pico da Torre ■

Câmara de Lobos

0   1   2   3   4   5 km

A   B

Brightly painted fishing boats in Câmara de Lobos

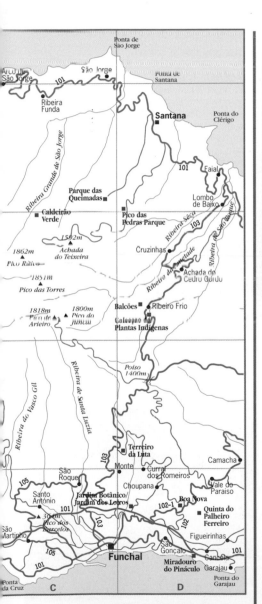

Cultivated terraces and densely planted fields create a sea of emerald green around Arco de São Jorge

61

What to See in Central Madeira

CABO GIRÃO (➤ 17, TOP TEN)

CÂMARA DE LOBOS ✪✪

The much-photographed fishing village of Câmara de Lobos owes its appeal to the small fleet of fishing boats based here, brightly painted in primary colours and drawn up on the town's small pebble beach for much of the day. On the eastern side of the harbour there is a small boatyard where you can watch boats being made and repaired. Local fishermen go out at night to catch *espada* (scabbard fish), which live at depths of 800m or more (hence their big eyes, needed to see in the gloom). At night they come up to feed, and that is when they are most easily caught, using long lines, each with 150 or so hooks, baited with squid.

To see the catch being brought in you need to be up early: by 7AM most of the fish will have been cleaned and despatched to Funchal market. The fishermen, meanwhile, celebrate the night's catch by filling the local bars. Heavy drinking is blamed for the evident poverty that you will encounter in the village, especially in the alleys leading west from the harbour, where large families live in tiny single-roomed houses, crammed up against the cliff face. Here you will also find the simple fishermen's chapel, its walls painted with naïve scenes showing the Apostles fishing on the shores of Lake Galilee, and the miracles of St Nicholas, patron saint of seafarers. Further west, up the hill, is the larger Church of São Sebastião, with its *azulejos* and statue of the saint stuck with arrows.

✚ 60B1

✉ 14km west of Funchal

🍴 Good choice of cafés and restaurants (£–££), including Churchill's Place (££, ☎ 944 336), on the east side of the harbour

🚌 Most westbound buses go to Câmara de Lobos, including 4, 6, 107, 154

♿ None

↔ Cabo Girão (➤ 17)

❓ The Feast of St Peter the Fisherman is celebrated with a lively festival in Câmara de Lobos on 29 Jun

Sir Winston Churchill was among the artists who came to paint this view of Câmara de Lobos

Climbing Pico Ruivo

Getting to the top of Madeira's highest peak does not require exceptional skills in mountaineering since there is a good paved path all the way to the summit, but you do need to carry a light jacket as it can be cold on the mountain top, and you should take adequate precautions against sunburn.

Start early for the best panoramas: by the middle of the morning warm air rising from the coastal regions will have condensed on meeting the colder air of the mountains, forming clouds that, although lending their own charm to the scene, limit the views.

A spectacular ridge-top footpath links Pico Ruivo and Pico do Arieiro

To reach the path, drive from Santana (➤ 70) along the EN 101–5 to the car park and rest house where the road runs out at Achada do Teixeira (1,592m).

Just behind the rest house is the curious rock formation known as Homem em Pé (Man on Foot), a group of eroded basalt dykes.

The well-trodden path to Pico Ruivo (Red Peak) leads west from here. After some 45 minutes, the path divides; take the path to the right up through a gate and on to the government rest house, a prominent white building. Two minutes on, the path divides and you take the left fork.

From here it is a scramble over rough boulder steps to the Pico Ruivo summit (1,861m), but the effort is well worth while for the breathtaking views of the central mountain range, and of the island of Porto Santo (➤ 85), floating in the sea away to the northeast.

Distance
3.5km

Time
2 hours

Start/end point
Achada do Teixeira rest house
➕ 61C3
🚕 Taxi required

Lunch
Nearest café is in Santana; drinks (coffee, beer, cola etc) can be bought at the rest house just below the summit

*The impressive coastal
landscape at Faial*

CURRAL DAS FREIRAS (➤ 18, TOP TEN)

FAIAL   ✪

Faial is worth a brief stop for the views to be had from the *miradouro* (viewpoint) overlooking the Ametade Valley, west of the village. In the centre of the village is the new bridge that replaced one swept away in flash floods in 1980, spanning the Ribeira Séca (Dry River) which lives up to its name most of the time but can rise to a raging torrent with the autumn rains. The *miradouro* west of the village is the best spot to take in the gaunt heights of Penha de Águia (Eagle Rock), the peak that overshadows Faial, rising sheer from the sea to a height of 590m.

MONTE   ✪✪✪

High above Funchal, the hill town of Monte is now easily reached thanks to the new cable car that runs from the Zona Velha (➤ 111).

Quite apart from the famous Monte toboggan ride (➤ 21), there are several good reasons for coming to Monte. One is to visit the Church of Nossa Senhora (Our Lady), whose spotlit façade is a prominent landmark at night, visible on the hillside high above Funchal. The pleasing classical building, its grey basalt detailing contrasted with whitewashed walls, is reached by climbing up a steep flight of 74 stone steps. Penitents scramble up these steps on their knees during the festivities for the Feast of the Assumption (15 August). Inside the church is a precious statue of the Virgin housed in a silver tabernacle. It is said that the 15th-century statue was given to a Madeiran shepherd girl by the Virgin herself, and it is credited with many miracles. The north chapel contains the imposing black coffin of the Emperor Charles I (➤ 14), who died of pneumonia on Madeira in 1922, aged 35.

At the foot of the church steps is a stretch of cobbled road marking the start of the Monte toboggan ride, and toboggan drivers hang about here, in their uniform of white shirt and trousers, leather boots and straw hat, waiting for customers. The luxuriant Jardim do Monte municipal garden stands to the north of the steps, built around a short stretch of railway viaduct, now smothered in tropical greenery. The viaduct is a vestige of the rack-and-pinion railway that once linked Monte to Funchal. Having opened in 1894 to take tourists up and down, the railway was closed after an accident in 1939, when an engine blew up, killing four people. The station building survives on the

main square above, the Largo do Fonte, where an ancient plane tree shelters the waiting taxi drivers.

In the opposite direction, it is a short walk to the excellent **Monte Palace Tropical Garden**, laid out over 7ha of lush hillside. Children will enjoy exploring the garden's maze of paths leading to fishponds, grottoes and bridges, Japanese-style gates and gushing fountains.

PICO DO ARIEIRO (► 23, TOP TEN)

The steps of Monte's Nossa Senhora church, which pilgrims climb on their knees

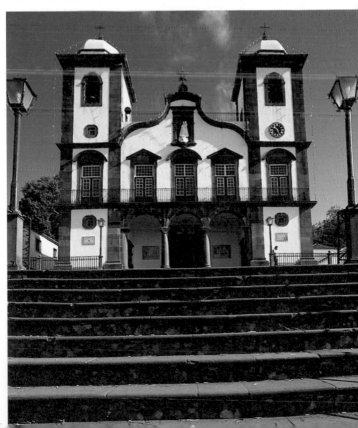

*Above: on a sheltered
plain, Ponta Delgada
basks by the sea*

PONTA DELGADA

The beachside church in Ponta Delgada contains the charred figure of the crucified Christ, which is taken in procession round the village during one of Madeira's biggest religious festivals, celebrated on the first Sunday in September. The miraculous figure was found washed up on the shore in the 16th century. In 1908 it survived a fire, which destroyed the rest of the church (now rebuilt). Across from the church is a rock-cut swimming pool, replenished by the tides and by Atlantic waves which dash against the walls showering bathers, much to the delight of children.

The neighbouring village of Boaventura stands in a humid and fertile valley where willow plantations supply the raw material for the island's wicker industry (➤ 76). The palm-shaded cemetery shelters the grave of Miss Turner (died 1925), who never visited the spot in her lifetime but desired to be buried here because of her gardener's vivid accounts of the area's scenic beauty.

RIBEIRO FRIO

Ribeiro Frio is a delightful spot set among scented woodland. Here the fresh clean waters of the Ribeiro Frio (meaning 'cold river') are channelled into a series of deep pools to create a small trout farm. Trout inevitably feature on the menu of the restaurant alongside. Woodland glades on the opposite side of the road are planted with flowering trees and shrubs to create a miniature botanical garden, where basking butterflies add to the colour.

Ribeiro Frio is the meeting point of several *levada* walks. One of the easiest is the walk to Balcões, which you can pick up by walking downhill from the trout farm and taking the broad track to the left that leads to the *levada*. Follow the wide level path for about 10 minutes to reach Balcões, whose name (meaning 'balcony') becomes obvious when you arrive: stunning landscapes open up from this hillside viewpoint across the sun-dappled Ametade Valley to the Penha de Águia (Eagle Rock), on Madeira's northern coast. The *levada* continues for another 2km, with views of the bare volcanic peaks around Pico do Arieiro (➤ 23). On the opposite side of the road is Levada do Furado, signposted to Portela. If you walk as far as the bridge over the River Bezerro (allow an hour) you will experience a sequence of splendid views across central Madeira's mountainous green interior.

Going nowhere tish swirl endlessly in Ribeira Frio's spring-fed trout farm

TERREIRO DA LUTA ★

Terreiro da Luta consists of a massive monument to the Virgin, illuminated at night and visible from downtown Funchal. The monument was erected in 1927 in thanksgiving after German submarines, seeking to end the use of the island as a supply base, sank several ships and started shelling Funchal in 1916. The bombardment ceased after prayers to the Virgin. The massive chains surrounding the monument come from the anchors of the Allied ships sunk in the harbour.

Across from the monument is the terminus of the Funchal to Monte railway, which closed in 1939 (➤ 64). From the terrace of this 1912 building there are good views down to Funchal.

 61D2
 8km north of Funchal
 Nearest cafés (£–££) in Monte, 2km south
Buses 103, 138
Monte (➤ 64)

In the Know

If you only have a short time to visit Madeira, or would like to get a real flavour of the island, here are some ideas:

10
Ways to Be a Local

Drink strong black espresso coffee (a *bica* in Portuguese) in the morning and tea (*cha*) in the afternoon.

Learn some basic Portuguese, if only to say *bom dia*, *boa tarde* and *boa noite* (good morning, afternoon and evening).

Shop early for freshly baked bread and the best choice of fruit, vegetables, flowers and fish.

Go for an early evening stroll with your friends along the Avenida Arriaga, or go window shopping in the streets around the cathedral in Funchal.

Go out again after dinner to meet your friends in cafés or bars around the Zona Velha and the cathedral in Funchal, and stay up late.

Take a long siesta to catch up on last night's lost sleep.

Go crazy over televised football in any bar, or live

at Funchal's stadium, the home ground of C S Marítimo, Madeira's first-division team.

Join a village festival, often advertised by the explosive sound of fire-crackers being detonated.

Wear a bobble hat with ear flaps as protection from the wind when walking in the mountains.

Travel by bus to savour a cross-section of Madeiran society.

10
Good Places to Have Lunch

Arsénio's (££) ✉ Rua de Santa Maria 169 ☎ 224 007. Come here to listen to genuine *fado* music while you eat.

Bio Logos (£) ✉ Rua Nova São Pedro ☎ 236 868. Good fresh salads and vegetables are hard to find on Madeiran menus so eat healthily and help to keep this small wholefood and vegetarian restaurant in business.

Café do Teatro (£) ✉ Teatro Baltazar Dias, Avenida Arriaga ☎ 236 400. The most chic young Funchalese poseurs and artistic types come here, with the aim of being seen by their friends. Cool black and white décor and a pretty cobbled patio garden.

Café Esplenada Arco-Velha (£) ✉ Rua de Carlos I 42. Enjoy a simple but satisfying lunch of

limpets and grilled sardines at this Old Town restaurant and watch the world go by from its pavement tables.

Golden Gate (£) ✉ Avenida Arriaga 21 ☎ 220 053. Usually packed with Funchalese office workers, shoppers and people killing time before the bus home, this is the place where local people go for a snack.

Jardim do Carreira (£) ✉ Rua do Carreira 118 ☎ 222 498. Seek out the attractive cobbled courtyard garden at the rear of this bar for some good inexpensive home cooking.

Jasmin Tea House (£) ✉ Quinta da Ribeira, Caminho dos Pretos 40, São Gonçalo, Funchal ☎ 792 796. The lazy way to get to this house in the woods is to take a taxi or bus 47. Most visitors come here by walking from the Quinta do Palheiro gardens (at the garden exit turn right, follow the estate wall up hill, turn left in the village and walk up about 100m to a white garage, then turn left up a track to the *levada* path. Follow the *levada* path for 25 minutes through eucalyptus woods and you will work up the necessary appetite to enjoy the home-made salads, soups and sandwiches served here at lunchtime – or the cream teas – prepared by the friendly English owners, Roy and Denise Chambers.

Nuns' Valley Café (£)
✉ Curral das Freiras
☎ 712 177. Lunch with one of Madeira's finest views: chestnuts are the local speciality so try chestnut bread or soup (and chestnut liqueur for those who are not driving).

Quinta do Magnólia (££)
✉ Rua do Dr Pita
☎ 704 013. Spoil yourself, without paying a fortune, by being a guinea pig for the catering students at the Quinta Magnólia Hotel School (reservations essential – book at least a day in advance).

Vagrant (Beatles' Boat) (££) ✉ Avenida das Comunidades Madeirenses ☎ 223 572. Spoil your children with lunch on this novelty boat and try explaining to them who the Beatles were, and why they were important.

Diving among tuna; why not use your time in Madeira to gain a scuba-diving certificate?

10
Top Activities

***Levada* walking**: it is what makes Madeira different and special; buy the Sunflower walking guide for lots of ideas.

Being botanical: you cannot visit Madeira without being bowled over by nature's profusion; buy a guide to the flora of Madeira and discover the names of all those beautiful flowering trees.

Wine tasting: learn the difference between the different types of Madeira wine by taking advantage of the free tastings offered by many wine shops and cellars.

Keeping fit: many people come to Madeira just to keep fit by swimming and playing tennis, making the most of the hotel sports facilities.

Learning geology: Madeira has a classic volcanic landscape, which you can study with the aid of a good introduction to geology.

Shopping for embroidery: even if you decide you cannot afford that gorgeous embroidered blouse, or that lovely nightdress, you can at least dream.

Sailing: surrounded by water, Madeira is the ideal place to enjoy a short coastal voyage.

Diving: learn to dive with the Dive College International, based in the Hotel Dom Pedro Baía in Machico (☎ 965 751).

Fishing: try your hand at catching marlin, swordfish or barracuda (➤ 112).

Golf: Madeira has two of Europe's most scenic links (➤ 112–13).

5
Good Places to Swim

• The Lido (➤ 111)
• Porto Santo – one huge stretch of golden sand (➤ 85)
• Prainha, Madeira's sandiest beach (➤ 80)
• Santa Cruz – the other sandy beach on Madeira, little visited by anyone but locals
• The Savoy Hotel

5
Good Viewpoints

• Pico do Arieiro (➤ 23)
• Pico Ruivo (➤ 63)
• Boca da Encumeada (➤ 50)
• The Eira do Serrado above Curral das Freiras (➤ 18–19)
• The cliff tops at Ponta de São Lourenço (➤ 81)

69

➕ 61D4
✉ Santana lies 42km north of Funchal
🍴 Several cafés and restaurants (£–££)
🚌 Buses 103, 132, 138
♿ None
💷 Free
↔ Pico Ruivo (► 63)

Drying maize in Santana and (below) inside a triangular house

SANTANA ✪✪✪

Santana presents a picture of domestic and agricultural prosperity. Here the predominant colours are the greens of terraced fields and hay meadows, interspersed by apple, pear and cherry orchards. Dotted among the haystacks and the pollarded willows are triangular thatched buildings, used by local farmers as cow byres. Here cattle are tethered for their own safety (to prevent them from tumbling on the steep hillsides), and to provide them with cool shade in summer and shelter from winter's wind.

Traditionally, people have lived in these ingenious structures too. Many are neglected and decaying, but a government scheme to encourage their restoration means

that several in Santana are still inhabited. With their brightly painted triangular façades and a roof that sweeps from the ridge to the ground, these highly distinctive A-framed buildings are unique to this part of the island. They are also surprisingly spacious, as you will discover if you visit the souvenir shop in the centre of Santana, where a typical A-frame house, called a *palheiros*, has been faithfully restored.

The EN 101-5 road south leads to Achada do Teixeira, from where you can walk to Pico Ruivo (► 63), Madeira's highest peak. Further north a rough minor road leads to the government rest house at Queimadas. This marks the start of one of Madeira's finest *levada* walks, taking in spectacular ravines and primeval forest. The ultimate goal (reached after about an hour) is the 300m-high waterfall that cascades into the pool at the bottom of the well-named fern- and moss-filled Caldeirão Verde (Green Cauldron).

Around Central Madeira

This drive takes a whole day, encompassing fishing ports and wave-battered cliffs, green valleys and volcanic peaks.

Start early and head for Câmara de Lobos (➤ 62), hoping to catch the last of the bustle surrounding the town's fish market. Continue to Cabo Girão (➤ 17) for a dizzying peep over the top of Europe's second highest sea cliff.

At Ribeira Brava (➤ 54) you can enjoy a reviving cup of coffee in a seafront café before exploring the Manueline Church of São Bento.

Drive north up the terraced slopes of the valley of the Ribeira Brava to Boca da Encumeada (➤ 50) for views of the northern and southern coast of Madeira. Descend through woodland to São Vicente (➤ 56) and then follow the meandering north coast eastwards.

You may want to stop and swim at Ponta Delgada (➤ 66) before continuing on to Santana (➤ 70) for lunch, shopping, or to explore the triangular houses.

If you are feeling energetic, consider climbing Pico Ruivo (➤ 63). Alternatively, continue to Faial (➤ 64) and drive south to Ribeiro Frio (➤ 66) for a gentle stroll to Balcões. A third option is to continue on to the Poiso pass and drive west to the summit of Pico do Arieiro (➤ 23). From the Poiso pass the road descends via Terreiro da Luta (➤ 67) to Monte (➤ 64), where you can explore the Monte Palace Tropical Garden (open till 6, closed Sundays) before the short drive back to Funchal.

Distance
120km

Time
8 hours

Start/end point
Funchal
✚ 61C1

Lunch
O Virgílio (£)
✉ São Vicente
☎ 842 467

This gilded woodwork on the altar of Câmara de Lobos church is typical of Madeiran churches

Eastern Madeira

Although the landscapes of eastern Madeira are tamer than those of the central mountain range, they are not without their own drama, especially along the eastern spur where the island tails off in a sequence of wild cliffs and rocky islets dashed by the Atlantic waves. Inland there are lush green river valleys, some turned into manicured golf courses, others carved into tiny plots for growing fruit and vegetables. The modern face of Madeira is represented by Santa Catarina and the free port at Caniçal, not to mention the tower blocks and holiday complexes of Madeira's second biggest town, Machico. A taste of Madeira's past survives at Caniçal, with its tuna-fishing fleet and Whaling Museum, and at Camacha, the centre of the island's wicker-weaving industry. As always on Madeira, the north coast is the place to go for solitude and a respite from modernity.

> '*Madeira's seasons are the youth, maturity and old age of a never-ending, still-beginning Spring.*'
>
> H N COLERIDGE
> *Six Months in the West Indies*
> (1825)

———————●———————

Tuna boats bob in Machico harbour

Looking down from Machico's Pico do Facho (Beacon Hill)

EASTERN MADEIRA

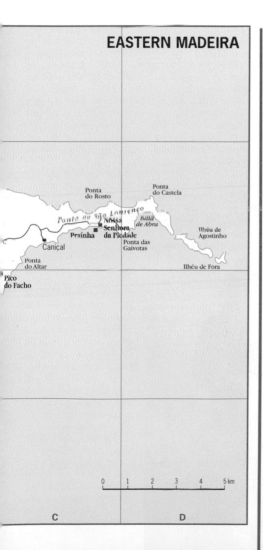

Ponta
do Rosto

Ponta
do Castela

Ponta de São Lourenço

Nossa
Senhora
da Piedade

Baía
de Abra

Prainha

Caniçal

Ponta das
Gaivotas

Ilhéu de
Agostinho

Ponta
do Altar

Ilhéu de Fora

Pico
do Facho

0   1   2   3   4   5 km

C

D

Pink hydrangeas form the
field boundary in
Machico's fertile valley

What to See in Eastern Madeira

CAMACHA ✪✪✪

74A2
16km northeast of Funchal
Buses 29, 77
Few.

The village of Camacha sits on a high plateau to the northeast of Funchal. To enjoy the panoramic views to be had from this elevated position, you have to visit the café called O Relógio (The Clock), on the main square. This former *quinta* (rural mansion) sports a squat clock tower, whose clock and bell were brought here from Liverpool in 1896 by the philanthropical Dr Michael Grabham. The eclectic and highly accomplished Grabham was an expert, among other things, on Madeiran flora, tropical fish, organs, clocks, volcanoes and electro-magnetism; once asked how he could speak with such erudition on so many subjects, he replied: 'What I do not know, I make up'.

In addition to the café and restaurant, O Relógio is the largest outlet on the island for Madeira's distinctive wicker products. Baskets and furniture of all descriptions fill every inch of available space – hanging from the ceilings as well as being piled on the floors – and nobody will pressurise you to buy as you explore the packed rooms.

O Relógio

Largo da Achada, Camacha
Open daily 9–6, except public hols
922 777
Café (£) on the ground floor of O Relógio

Wicker is produced from the pollarded willows which thrive in the warm and humid valleys around Camacha. Cut back to a stunted and knobbly trunk each winter, the willows put out whip-like shoots, called osiers, up to 3m in length. The osiers are placed in tanks and soaked in water until the bark is sufficiently pliable to be peeled from the core. Great conical bundles of osiers are then delivered to the cottages of wicker-workers, who boil the canes to make them supple (this also changes the colour from white to tan) before weaving them into everything imaginable, from simple place mats and wastepaper baskets, to peacock-backed chairs or ornate birdcages.

Basket weaving looks easier than it is, when demonstrated by skilled wicker-workers

Demonstrations of wicker-weaving can sometimes be seen in the O Relógio basement, while the middle floor has a display of Noah's Ark animals and a galleon made by local weavers to show off their considerable skills.

CANIÇAL ⭐⭐

Caniçal was the centre of southern Europe's last whaling station until 1981, when the trade was banned by international treaty. Instrumental in the process of achieving the ban was the Society for the Protection of Marine Mammals, which helped establish the small but informative **Museu de Baleia** (Whaling Museum), now located in the offices once used by the Caniçal whaling company. Videos and displays in the museum explain how retired Madeiran fishermen have turned from whale hunting to conservation, putting their knowledge of sperm whale habits and migration patterns at the disposal of marine biologists who hope to establish a marine mammal sanctuary around Madeira.

The brightly coloured boats drawn up on the pebbly shore alongside the museum belong to Madeira's biggest tuna fleet; it is fascinating to stand and watch the fishermen maintaining and repairing them, using timeless craft techniques.

🔶 75C3
✉ 32km east of Funchal
🍴 Café (£) next to museum and along the seafront
🚌 Bus 113
♿ Few
↔ Machico (► 79)

Museu de Baleia
✉ Largo da Lota
☎ 961 407
🕐 Tue–Sun 10–12, 1–6. Closed Mon
✋ Moderate

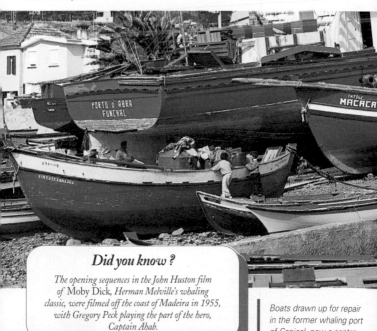

Did you know ?

The opening sequences in the John Huston film of Moby Dick, Herman Melville's whaling classic, were filmed off the coast of Madeira in 1955, with Gregory Peck playing the part of the hero, Captain Ahab.

Boats drawn up for repair in the former whaling port of Caniçal, now a centre for conservation studies

✚ 74A1
✉ 8km east of Funchal
🍴 Isidro café (££, ☎ 934 342) next to the church
🚌 Buses 2, 109, 110, 155
♿ Few
↔ Garajau (➤ below)

CANIÇO ✪

Caniço is a sprawling village of two parts: the old town is set inland, with attractive buildings surrounding the tree-shaded main square, including the 18th-century baroque church; while to the south a winding road leads to a number of cliff-top resort complexes, built here to take advantage of the sun and the sea views. Non-residents can pay to use the pool and sea-bathing facilities at the Roca Mar Hotel, and the clear waters here are popular with divers. Local people come to swim off the rocky beach at Praia dos Reis Magos, a short walk to the east.

✚ 74A1
✉ 8km east of Funchal
🍴 Snack Bar O Neptuno at the lower end of Garajau's main street, on the opposite side of the road to the Dom Pedro Hotel
🚌 Buses 2, 109, 110, 155
♿ Few
↔ Caniço (➤ above)

GARAJAU ✪

Garajau is Portuguese for 'tern', and the village is named after the attractive black-headed sea birds that nest on the nearby cliffs. As you explore the area, you may catch sight of these birds hovering over the limpid blue sea before plunging into the water to catch their food.

Garajau's most prominent landmark is the huge statue of Christ, erected here in 1927. Similar to the larger and more famous statues in Lisbon and Rio de Janeiro, it stands with outstretched arms on a headland 200m above the sea. From here you can walk down a cobbled track leading to the base of the cliffs, where a concrete causeway links a number of small boulder-strewn coves and beaches.

Garajau's cliffs are a favoured nesting site for acrobatic black-headed terns

MACHICO ✪✪✪

Machico is where Zarco first set foot on Madeira in 1420, claiming for Portugal an island that had been known to sailors for thousands of years. Among those who got to Madeira before Zarco were Robert Machin and Anne of Hereford, shipwrecked here after their storm-tossed ship was driven out into the Atlantic from the coast of Portugal. Robert and Anne died within days of each other and were buried by the rest of the crew, who later escaped by building a raft. On finding their graves some 50 years later, Zarco is said to have named the spot Machico, in Machin's honour (in fact, it is more likely that Machico is a corruption of Monchique, Zarco's home town in Portugal).

Zarco and his fellow navigator, Tristão Vaz Teixeira, were appointed governors of Madeira in 1425, with Zarco ruling the west from Funchal, and Teixeira in charge of the east, based in Machico. It is his statue that stands in front of the town's large 15th-century parish church.

The smaller Capela dos Milagres (Chapel of the Miracles), standing to the east of the town, is reputed to be built on the site of Machin's grave. The original church was washed away by flash floods in 1803, but the beautiful Gothic crucifix from the high altar was found floating at sea and returned by an American sailor.

Machico's third church (now locked and derelict) was built in 1739 to honour São Roque after he was believed to have answered the townspeople's prayers and saved them from plague. It stands on the western arm of Machico's wide bay, beyond the fish market and the triangular fortress, built in 1706, which has been restored to house the town's tourist office.

🔲 74B2

✉️ 24km northeast of Funchal

🍴 Several cafés and restaurants in Rua do Mercado (Market Street), including the Mercado Velho restaurant (£, ☎ 962 370) and the Pastelaria Galã café (£, ☎ 965 720)

🚌 Buses 20, 23, 53, 78, 113, 156

❓ Festa di Santissimo Sacramento (Feast of the Holy Sacrament), celebrated on the last weekend in Aug; procession in honour of Nosso Senhora de Milagres (Our Lord of Miracles) 8–9 October,

ℹ️ Forte de Nossa Senhora do Amparo (☎ 962 289, 🕐 Mon–Fri 9–12:30, 2–5; Sat 9–12)

♿ Few

↔️ Prainha (➤ 80)

Come to Machico in August for the carnival

*Idyllic Porto da Cruz
encourages relaxation as
it basks in the sun*

🕂 74A3
✉ 30km northeast of Funchal
🍴 Restaurant and tea house (£) at Faial
🚌 Buses 53, 78, 103
♿ Few
↔ Faial (► 64)

PORTO DA CRUZ   ✪

Porto da Cruz was once an important harbour town on the north coast of Madeira, thriving in an era when goods were transported from place to place by boat, but declining into a quiet backwater once motorised road transport took over. Today, the harbour that once buzzed with cargo boats is used as a diving platform by local children.

The port is reached by following the road that skirts the small fortress-crowned hill to the east of the village, past the sandy beach, on the left, and the sugar mill and distillery, on the right. The mill stands locked and unused for much of the year, but a sweet toffee-like scent fills the air during the sugar harvesting season – March, April and May – when production of *aguardente*, a rum-like spirit made from crushed sugar cane, is under way.

Something of the gloom that visitors to Porto da Cruz claim to experience is due to the shadows cast by Penha de Águia (Eagle Rock), rising to a height of 590m to the west of the village. The road to the east of the village gives out at Lorano, and from here there are splendid views to be had from the cliff-top path.

🕂 75C3
✉ 30km east of Funchal
🍴 Bar (£), overlooking the beach
🚌 Bus 113 will take you to Caniçal, after which you must take a taxi or walk
♿ Few
↔ Caniçal (► 77)

PRAINHA   ✪✪

Prainha enjoys the unique distinction of having the largest natural sand beach on Madeira. Hidden from the road, the beach is signposted along the road from Caniçal to Ponta de São Lourenço, and is reached down some steps beneath a chapel-topped hill. The brown-black sand on the beach derives from the local rock, a curious mixture of crushed shell and volcanic debris, pulverised by tens of thousands of years of wave action. The sheltered south-facing beach enjoys good views of the easternmost tip of Madeira, as well as of aeroplanes flying into nearby Santa Catarina airport; it can be crowded in July and August.

To Ponta de
São Lourenço

Follow this switchback path to the easternmost tip of Madeira and you will feel as if you are standing on the edge of the world.

To reach the start of the walk, drive east along the EN 101-3 through Caniçal (▶ 77) and past Prainha beach (▶ 80), until you come to the car park at the end of the tarmac road. Park here and set off along the path that starts by the big boulders at the eastern end of the car park, keeping right and heading downhill to the bottom of a shallow valley, then up the other side.

To your right is the great rocky sweep of the Baía de Abra (Abra Bay), with its towering orange and brown cliffs. Beyond the bay is Ilhéu de Fora, with its lighthouse, and an eyelet in the rock called Ponta do Furado. Further out to sea are the flat-topped Ilhas Desertas, inhabited only by seabirds and a small colony of protected monk seals.

After 20 minutes or so, the uphill track meets a boulder wall, with a gap for walkers to pass through. Bear left on a rocky path and descend to the valley where the path splits.

Go left to reach a viewpoint high above three purple rocks known as the 'seahorses', with a stunning westwards view of high cliffs and raging seas.

Return to the main path and head left towards the skyline. This will take you to another viewpoint with breathtaking views. Brave souls with a good head for heights can continue from here to the tip of Madeira, but the way lies over bare rocks with no visible path (red paint splodges and cairns act as a guide), and for most visitors the first viewpoint will be far enough.

Distance
2km

Time
1½ hours

Start/end point
Car park at easternmost end of EN 101-3 road, beyond Caniçal
✛ 75C3

Lunch
No café nearby but a caravan in the car park sells drinks; take a picnic

The Ilhas Desertas, inhabited only by seals and birds, lie off Madeira's south-western coast

Santa Cruz glories in this fine Town Hall and Law Court, with its basalt-grey balusters

QUINTA DO PALHEIRO FERREIRO (► 24, TOP TEN)

SANTA CRUZ ★

The people of Santa Cruz get an intimate view of aeroplanes coming into land at nearby Santa Catarina airport, which opened in 1964, but the town retains the peaceful atmosphere of a bygone era. The parish church of 1479 is one of the oldest on the island and echoes of Funchal's cathedral suggest that the same architect – Pedro Enes – could have been involved in the design. Three blocks east of the main square, in Rua da Ponta Nova, is the 19th-century Law Court with its splendid verandas and stone stairway. Flowering trees fill the park surrounding the court, while date palms and dragon trees line the seafront road, two blocks south, lending the pebble beach the air of an upmarket Riviera. Strung out along the promenade are cafés, the village market, the Municipal Library with a small art gallery and an open-air theatre, plus the Palm Beach lido, with paddling pools, a swimming pool and sea-bathing facilities.

SANTO ANTÓNIO DA SERRA ★

Aptly described as a Madeiran version of the English Home Counties, the wooded slopes around Santo António da Serra are dotted with the elegant mansions of the English merchants who once dominated the Madeira wine trade. Privacy, and a climate several degrees cooler than downtown Funchal, made this a favoured summer retreat. One splendid mansion, the Quinta da Serra, stands at the centre of a large public park where there are a few animal enclosures and a playground. The park is at its most colourful during the spring and early summer when the first flush of camellias is superseded by the bright blooms of azaleas. Avenues running through the park lead to a viewpoint that looks out to the easternmost tip of the island.

Santa Cruz
+ 74B2
✉ 17km east of Funchal
🍴 Cafés along the seafront (£) serving home-made cakes
🚌 Buses 20, 23, 53, 78, 113, 156
♿ Few
↔ Caniçal (► 77)

Santo António da Serra
+ 74A2
✉ 22km northeast of Funchal
🍴 Café (£) on the main square
🚌 Buses 20, 77, 78
♿ Few
↔ Camacha (► 76)
❓ Park open daily during daylight hours

Around Eastern Madeira

Allow at least half a day for this leisurely drive around Madeira's eastern spur, including time to swim off one of the island's few naturally sandy beaches.

Leave Funchal on the EN 101, following signs to the airport, then turn left, after 3km, on to the EN 102 signposted to Camacha.

After 2km turn right to visit the Blandy wine merchant family's splendid Quinta do Palheiro Ferreiro gardens (➤ 24).

Rejoin the EN 102 and continue north to Camacha (➤ 76). Continue along the EN 102 for a further 11km to Santo António da Serra.

At Santo António da Serra take a stroll in the park surrounding the Quinta da Serra (➤ 82), the home of the Blandy family before they acquired the Quinta do Palheiro Ferreiro.

Continue along the EN 101 but turn left, before reaching Machico, on the EN 101-3 signposted to Caniçal. Skirt Caniçal and continue to the end of the road for a walk out across the cliff tops at Ponta do São Lourenço (➤ 80).

Cool off from your walk by taking a dip in the sea at Prainha beach (➤ 80) on the way back to Caniçal, with its Whaling Museum (➤ 77). Stop at Machico (➤ 79), Madeira's second town, to walk around the bay and visit the three historic churches.

Follow the coastal road beneath the airport runway to Santa Cruz (➤ 82).

Depending on the time of day, your last stop before returning to Funchal could be Garajau (➤ 78), where you can watch the sun go down from the cliff top alongside the outsize statue of Christ.

Distance
60km

Time
6 hours

Start/end point
Funchal
✚ 61C1

Lunch
Marina (££)
✉ Rua do Leiria
☎ 966 625

Reminiscent of Rio's famous landmark, Madeira's own statue of Christ stands on the cliffs near Garajau

Porto Santo

Porto Santo is all about sun, sea and sand, and almost nothing else. The sleepy island is virtually flat, and there is little agriculture since Porto Santo lacks Madeira's abundant supplies of water. The island's population of 5,000 earns much of its living during July and August, when a steady stream of visitors arrives to soak up the sun and dance the night away in hotel discos. Some take the relatively expensive 15-minute flight from Madeira, while most risk seasickness on the catamaran that makes the 90-minute journey across the 37km of choppy ocean separating the two islands. Plans are afoot to develop Porto Santo's tourism further, with a golf course and resort hotels, but for the time being one of its chief attractions is that its magnificent sweep of beach remains clean, unspoilt and undeveloped.

> ' *The ancient cannon (some of which had fallen from their carriages) were emblems of peace rather than war, and fit subjects for a society of antiquaries.* '
>
> T E BOWDITCH, in a letter describing the residence of Porto Santo's governor in 1823

Porto Santo, famous for its beaches

What to See on Porto Santo

FONTE DA AREIA

The little rain that Porto Santo receives rapidly filters through the island's sandy soils to emerge as a series of springs when the water meets impermeable basalt. The Fonte da Areia (Spring in the Sand) is one such spring, and its popularity is guaranteed by the belief that drinking its waters restores body and soul and bestows longevity. For those who prefer alternative restoratives, there is a bar alongside the public drinking fountain, with palm-shaded tables creating a tropical illusion. The spring itself fills a series of troughs that were once used by local women for washing their laundry. The nearby cliffs of compressed sand have been eroded into bizarre sculptures by wind and rain, and there are rock pools to explore on the pebbly beach below. The spring can be reached on foot by taking the road west from Camacha; the Fonte da Areia makes a good destination for a day trip and, perhaps, a picnic.

86B3

3km northwest of Vila Baleira

Café (£) alongside the spring

Few

Vila Baleira (➤ 88)

PONTA DA CALHETA ✪

This southernmost tip of Porto Santo marks the watershed between the long sweep of sandy beach running along the southern coast of the island and the rocky northern coast. A good time to come here is dusk, when the setting sun casts shadows and colours over the much-eroded rocks on the offshore islands, allowing you to exercise your imagination and see all sorts of shapes. The evening can be extended by taking a meal of fresh fish in the nearby restaurant, then walking back along the sandy beach while imagining you are in your own private paradise.

➕ 86A1
✉ 5km southwest of Vila Baleira
🍴 Pôr-do-Sol restaurant (£££, ☎ 984 380) at the point where the coastal road ends
♿ Few
↔ Vila Baleira (➤ 88)

PORTELA ✪

The *miradouro* (viewpoint) at Portela may not be the highest point on Porto Santo, but it is the best place to get a sense of the scale of the pure sandy beach that seems to stretch endlessly along the southern coast. It will also give you an idea of why Porto Santo is known as the 'tawny island'. Deforestation at a very early stage in the island's history led to rapid erosion of the fertile topsoil, leaving the sand-coloured landscape you see today.

➕ 86C2
✉ 1.6km northeast of Vila Baleira
♿ Few
↔ Vila Baleira (➤ 88)

SERRA DO DENTRO ✪

The landscape of the Serra do Dentro Valley, forming the eastern part of the island, looks like the setting for a Wild West movie with its arid sheep- and cattle-grazed slopes. The terraces, abandoned farmhouses and threshing floors are all that remain of communities that gave up the struggle to scratch a living from the thin soil, while reservoirs and stunted tree saplings indicate government schemes to restore life to the area.

➕ 86C3
✉ 5km northeast of Vila Baleira
♿ Few
↔ Vila Baleira (➤ 88)

Did you know ?

The people of Porto Santo are known as profetas *(prophets) because one of their number declared himself to be a messenger from God in the 16th century. Madeirans are known, in their turn, as* americanos, *because the people of Porto Santo consider them wealthy and flash.*

Above: *not quite the Sahara, but Porto Santo does have enough sand to satisfy any beach connoisseur*

86B2

✉ On the southern coast of Porto Santo, 10 minutes' drive from the airport

🍴 The Baiana café (£, ☎ 984 649), on Largo do Pelourinho, serves excellent grilled fish

♿ Few

ℹ Rua Dr Vieira da Castro (☎ 982 361)

Casa Museu Cristóvão Colombo

☎ 983 405

🕐 Tue–Fri 10–6, Sat, Sun, public hols 10–1

Christopher Columbus lived in a house close to this church

VILA BALEIRA ⊙⊙

Vila Baleira is Porto Santo's capital, and it is here that most of the 5,000 inhabitants live. The town was founded by Bartolomeu Perestrelo, the island's first governor, who did not draw the short straw you might think from the island's present appearance: in the 15th century it was a profitable colony, producing cereals, wines and sugar, as well as dyestuffs from the sap of dragon trees.

Two dragon trees survive in the town's main square, Largo do Pelourinho, flanking the entrance to the 16th-century Town Hall. Alongside is the popular Bar Gel Burger, the centre of the island's social life. To the north is the much-restored parish church, with only a small side chapel surviving from the 15th-century Gothic original. From opposite the Town Hall, Rua Infante D Henrique, the town's palm-lined main street, leads straight to the beach, the objective of most visitors.

In the street behind the church is the **Casa Museu Cristóvão Colombo**, reputed to be the house in which Christopher Columbus lived during his stay on Porto Santo (▶ 14). There is a good library of books in English, Portuguese and other languages, from which you can learn all there is to know about the famous Genoese explorer, and several imaginative portraits and amusing prints depict the arrival of some of the first Europeans to land on American shores.

Did you know ?

The grapes grown on Porto Santo ripen early, baked by the warmth of the sun reflected from the island's sandy soil. They taste very sweet, and are used to make verdelho, *the excellent (and very alcoholic) local wine.*

Along the Sands of Porto Santo

You can take a couple of hours to walk the 6.5km from Vila Baleira to Ponta da Calheta, or you can spend all day, stopping to swim, sunbathe or laze around in beach cafés.

Follow Avenue Dr M Pestana Junior, the coastal road, westwards out of Vila Baleira. Shortly after passing the church of Espirito Santo, at Campo de Baixo, turn right up a road signposted to Pedreira (Quarry).

Occasionally you will pass ruined farm buildings and the stumps and stone towers of ancient windmills surviving from the time when wheat was grown on Porto Santo. The quarry, when you reach it, has exposed rock patterned like organ pipes.

The road – really a potholed track – continues round the low hill called Pico de Ana Ferreira (283m), and rejoins the coast road at Ponta. Turn right at Ponta and continue until the road runs out at Ponta da Calheta.

The café here is a good spot to enjoy a long lazy lunch and views that, on a clear day, stretch to Madeira.

Afterwards, you can take bus No. 4 back to Vila Baleira (last departure 6:20PM) or enquire at the Pôr-do-Sol about their free shuttle bus service. Alternatively, if you still have the energy, you can follow the sands back to Vila Baleira.

The beach remains idyllically unspoiled, with room for all comers, from windsurfers and sun worshippers to the Madeirans who bury themselves in the sands, believing them to have therapeutic properties.

Distance
6.5km

Time
2½ hours

Start/end point
Vila Baleira
✠ 86B2

Lunch
Pôr-do-Sol (£££)
✉ Ponta da Calheta
☎ 984 380

Whether you walk its whole length or just a short stretch, Porto Santo's beach is inviting and unspoiled

Around Porto Santo

Distance
15km

Time
3 hours

Start/end point
Vila Baleira
✚ 86B2

Lunch
Bar Torres (£)
✉ Camacha
☎ 984 373

Windmills, once used for grinding maize, are common on Porto Santo, though few are now in working condition

Take a taxi, or hire a car, for a half-day tour of Porto Santo's main sights.

From Vila Baleira follow Rua Bispo D E de Alencastre eastwards (signposted to Serra de Fora).

The road takes you to the viewpoint at Portela (➤ 87) and on to the farming villages of Serra da Fora and Serra do Dentro (➤ 87). The views change as you swing round the north side of the island to Camacha, with its restored windmill and the Estrela do Norte restaurant (➤ 99), which is housed in an old farmhouse and specialises in barbecued chicken.

In Camacha, take the minor road that leads to the Fonte da Areia to sample the waters, which are reputed to bestow eternal youth on those who drink them. Return to the main road and drive south for 2km, then turn left on the minor road that goes to the viewpoint on Pico do Castelo (437m).

From the cone-shaped peak there are sweeping views over the whole island, with the airport runway prominent in the plain to the west. On the summit you will find the scant remains of the fortification after which the Pico do Castelo is named. Islanders used to take refuge on those frequent occasions when pirates raided Vila Baleira. Warning bonfires were lit on the neighbouring hill, called Pico do Facho (Beacon Peak), the island's highest point at 517m.

You can walk from one peak to the other through pine plantations before heading back downhill for the short return stretch to Vila Baleira.

Where To...

Above: a tuna fish decorating a fishing boat
Right: history in a bottle: vintage Madeira

Funchal

Prices
Prices are approximate, based on a three-course meal for one without drinks and service:

£ = under 15 euros
££ = 15–30 euros
£££ = 30 euros

Opening Hours
Most restaurants in Funchal open from 11 in the morning through to 11 at night. Smarter restaurants close between 3 and 7.

A Muralha (££)
As well as all the usual Madeiran specialities, A Muralha serves several more unusual regional dishes, including *picadinho* (fragrant herby stewed beef) and wild rabbit.

✉ **Largo do Corpo Santo 2** ☎ **232 561** ⓘ **Lunch, dinner**

A Rampa (££)
Located opposite the Savoy Hotel, A Rampa is a favourite with families, serving authentic pizzas and pasta dishes, including children's favourites such as macaroni and spaghetti Bolognese, as well as fresh salads and a range of more substantial fish and meat dishes, cooked Italian style. Friendly waiters and good-value prices.

✉ **Henry II Building 1st Floor, Avenida do Infante** ☎ **235 275** ⓘ **Lunch, dinner**

Arsénio's (££)
Funchal's long-established *fado* house attracts mainland Portuguese holiday-makers and *aficionados* of the plaintive doom-laden songs of the Lisbon back streets. Listen while you eat.

✉ **Rua de Santa Maria 169** ☎ **224 007** ⓘ **Lunch, dinner**

Bamboo Inn (££)
Good use is made of Madeira's unfailing supply of fresh fish and vegetables at this Chinese restaurant in the Hotel Zone – a good choice for when you cannot bear the idea of beef on a spit for dinner yet again.

✉ **Estrada Monumental 318, 2nd Floor** ☎ **766 861** ⓘ **Lunch, dinner**

Bio Logos (£)
Tiny café specialising in vegetarian and organic food. No menu – just a range of good fresh salads, quiches, pies, casseroles and pizzas. The choice diminishes as the day goes on.

✉ **Rua Nova São Pedro** ☎ **236 868** ⓘ **Lunch only**

Bombay Palace (££)
This excellent tandoori restaurant makes a welcome change from a diet of Madeiran sardines, kebabs and tuna. Try the tandoori fish for an unusual starter.

✉ **Eden Mar Shopping Centre, Rua do Gorgulho** ☎ **763 110** ⓘ **Lunch, dinner**

Casa Carochinha (££)
Carochinha markets itself to English visitors as a home from home, with its lace tablecloths, bread and butter pudding and roast beef, but the restaurant also features many typically Madeiran dishes. Good-value set lunch menu.

✉ **Rua de São Francesco 2** ☎ **223 695** ⓘ **Lunch, dinner**

Casa dos Reis (££)
Intimate dining room decorated with topographical prints of Madeira; ideal for romantic candle-lit suppers. Charcoal-grilled lamb and fish specialities.

✉ **Rua Impertriz Dona Amélia 101** ☎ **225 182** ⓘ **Lunch, dinner**

Casa Velha (£££)
Ceiling fans gently stir the air at this elegant restaurant – ideal for a special night out – set in a villa with flower-filled gardens. Specialises in *flambé* dishes and lobster.

✉ **Rua Imperatriz Dona Amélia 69** ☎ **205 600** ⓘ **Lunch, dinner**

Doca do Cavacas (££)

Not easily found (follow the road to the port and take the footpath beside the Duas Torres Hotel), this atmospheric restaurant enjoys magnificent sea views and specialises in fresh fish brought in by the fishing boats moored at the adjacent quay.

✉ Ponta da Cruz, Estrada Monumental ☎ 762 057 🕐 Lunch, dinner

Don Filet (££)

Beef is king at this restaurant round the corner from the Savoy Hotel, where you can eat your fillets Brazilian style, broiled over a charcoal grill, or Madeiran style, skewered on a bay twig and flavoured with garlic.

✉ Rua do Favilo 7 ☎ 764 426 🕐 Lunch, dinner. Closed Sun lunch

Dona Amélia (££)

An elegant and well-restored town house with a terrace garden makes an atmospheric setting for the international-style cuisine served here.

✉ Rua Imperatriz Dona Amélia 83 ☎ 225 784 🕐 Lunch, dinner

Les Faunes (£££)

Arguably Madeira's best restaurant, and the place to eat if expense is no object, serving top-quality international cuisine. The bright and airy dining room is simply decorated with Picasso drawings of fauns. Impeccable service. Though not as formal as Reid's Dining Room (➤ 102), you need to dress smartly. Reservations advised.

✉ Reid's Hotel, Estrada Monumental ☎ 717 171 🕐 Lunch, dinner

Fleur de Lys (£££)

For not much more than the cost of a meal in some of Funchal's downtown restaurants, you can treat yourself to the sophisticated ambience of the Savoy Hotel's flagship restaurant, while enjoying panoramic views over Funchal and the harbour. Reservations essential.

✉ Savoy Hotel, Avenida do Infante ☎ 222 031 🕐 Lunch, dinner

Gavião Novo (££)

This smart new restaurant in the Old Town specialises in fish. It is always worth asking the waiters what is best because they often have specials not listed on the main menu – it all depends what the fishermen who supply them have managed to hook.

✉ Rua Santa Maria 131 ☎ 229 238 🕐 Lunch, dinner

Hong Kong (££)

Authentic Cantonese-style food, from sweet and sour pork to squid with garlic and black beans, or steamed fish with ginger.

✉ Olimpo Shopping Centre, Avenida do Infante ☎ 228 181 🕐 Lunch, dinner

Le Jardin (££)

French influences are to be found in the cooking at this Old Town restaurant specialising in flambé fish and peppered steak.

✉ Rua de Carlos I 60 ☎ 222 864 🕐 Lunch, dinner

Kon Tiki (££)

After a week of meat kebabs and espada (scabbard fish), visitors seeking a change could do worse than visit the Kon Tiki restaurant for beef broiled on hot lava stones (Finnish style) or shark steak. Inevitably, espada is on offer too, but here the flamboyant waiters flambé the fish at your table with prawns.

✉ Rua do Favila 9 ☎ 764 737 🕐 Lunch, dinner

Taking a Taxi

If you take a taxi to a restaurant, be prepared for the taxi driver to try to persuade you to try a different establishment; they may tell you that they know a better and cheaper restaurant, very special and known only to locals. Take their advice if you wish, but be aware that the taxi driver is probably getting a commission from the restaurant, that it will often be out of town (hence the taxi driver earns a bigger fare for taking you there) and that if you do not like the restaurant or its prices there will probably not be a cheaper alternative in the neighbourhood.

Garlic Bread

When you sit down to eat in a Madeiran restaurant the waiter will probably present you with a basket of delicious home-made bread, spread with garlic butter and warmed in the oven – a delicious accompaniment to pre-dinner drinks while you contemplate the menu.

Fish on the Menu

Your favourite fish may not seem so familiar if the menu lists them in Portuguese only. Here is a short list of names that you will frequently find on Madeiran menus: *atum* is tuna; *bacalhau* is salted cod; *cherne* is sea bass; *carapau* is mackerel; *pargo* is bream; *salmão* is salmon; *salmonete* is red mullet; *truta* is trout; *espadarte* is swordfish (not to be confused with *espada*, the ubiquitous Madeiran speciality, scabbard fish).

Londres (££)

Despite the name, Londres specialises in mainland Portuguese dishes, including *bacalhau* (salt cod) for which there are said to be as many recipes as there are days in the year. Here they serve a different Portuguese speciality every day.

✉ **Rua da Carreira 64A** ☎ **235 329** 🕐 **Lunch, dinner. Closed Sun**

McDonald's (£) and Pizza Hut (££)

It had to happen sooner or later – Madeira now has its own McDonald's. What's more, there is a Pizza Hut next door, so for those of you with children who will not eat anything but fast food, here is the solution.

✉ **Avenida das Comunidades Madeirenses 1 (Pizza Hut) and 2 (McDonald's)** ☎ **800 221 122 (Pizza Hut takeaway and deliveries)** 🕐 **Lunch, dinner**

Mar Azul (££)

The Mar Azul is one of several restaurants running round the northern rim of Madeira's Yacht Marina. Do not be put off by the sight of keen waiters outside touting for business, possibly implying that this is a tourist rip-off joint. The food is excellent, as is the entertainment – Madeiran folk dancers perform authentic island dances on the pavement outside and even those who hate the idea of 'folk' will be charmed. Prices are reasonable so long as you avoid the lobster.

✉ **Funchal Yacht Marina, Avenida das Comunidades Madeirenses** ☎ **230 079** 🕐 **Lunch, dinner**

Marina Terrace (££)

Another waterside restaurant located on the northern rim of the Yacht Marina, serving everything from pizza to lobster. Staff are in Madeiran costume and there is live folk dancing on Monday and Saturday nights and *fado* music on Tuesdays, Thursdays and Sundays, from around 7:30.

✉ **Marina do Funchal** ☎ **230 547** 🕐 **Lunch, dinner**

Marisa (££)

When you visit this tiny Old Town restaurant you feel as if you are a guest in someone's home, as father and son cook delicious seafood and rice dishes while mother takes the orders and waits at table. Very good value.

✉ **Rua de Santa Maria 162** ☎ **226 189** 🕐 **Lunch, dinner**

Moby Dick (££)

Fish restaurant in the Hotel Zone serving a wide range of fresh fish, from *espada de camarão* (scabbard fish with prawns) to *atum con todos* (tuna with everything!).

✉ **Estrada Monumental 187** ☎ **776 868** 🕐 **Lunch, dinner**

O Almirante (££)

Walls decorated with paintings of ships and nautical memorabilia set the theme for this popular Old Town restaurant specialising in meat on the spit, fish and shellfish.

✉ **Largo do Poço 1–2** ☎ **224 252** 🕐 **Lunch, dinner**

O Celeiro (££)

The intimate Cellar restaurant is a good place to sample *caldeirada* (fish casserole) or the southern Portuguese speciality of *cataplana de mariscos* (seafood casserole).

✉ **Rua dos Aranhas 22** ☎ **230 622** 🕐 **Lunch, dinner**

O Jango (££)

This intimate Old Town restaurant, converted from a former fisherman's home, specialises in seafood. Fans return again and again for the *cataplana*, a hearty fish stew whose ingredients are never the same two days running – the contents depending on what the local fishermen who supply the restaurant have caught that day.

🖂 Rua de Santa Maria 166
☎ 221 280 🕓 Lunch, dinner. Closed 1–21 Jul

O Panorâmico (£££)

If you like music with your meal, this is the place to come. The flagship restaurant at the Pestana Carlton Park Hotel offers dinner dances and live entertainment every Wednesday and Saturday.

🖂 Pestana Carlton Park, Largo António Nobre ☎ 209 100
🕓 Dinner

O Tapassol (££)

A favourite of old Madeira hands, this Old Town restaurant has a tiny rooftop terrace for outdoor dining and a menu featuring less-usual dishes, such as wild rabbit in season and octopus casserole.

🖂 Rua Dom Carlos I 62
☎ 225 023 🕓 Lunch, dinner

Portão (££)

In a sheltered corner to the rear of the Corpo Santo chapel in the Old Town, Portão is a quieter and more intimate restaurant than those on the main drag. Choose between authentic Portuguese salt cod with boiled egg ('a bras') or push the boat out with grilled lobster or prawns in champagne sauce – but save space for delicious Zabaionne Madeira, the classic Italian dessert made with Madeira rather than Marsala.

🖂 Rua Portão de São Tiago 1
☎ 221 125 🕓 Lunch, dinner

Prince Albert (££)

Themed as a Victorian pub, with dark wood panelling and much cut glass, the Prince Albert tends to attract a mainly British crowd who enjoy the *bonhomie* of pub conversation. The dining room serves a range of good Portuguese and international food.

🖂 Rua Imperatriz Dona Amélia 86 ☎ 235 793 🕓 Lunch, dinner

Quinta Palmeira (£££)

This 19th-century *quinta* is a rare survivor of the elegant mansions that lined Avenida do Infante before the high-rise hotel blocks arrived. Eat in the elegant, mirrored dining room, or on the garden terrace, and choose from an extensive menu which includes several vegetarian dishes.

🖂 Avenida do Infante 5
☎ 221 814 🕓 Lunch, dinner

Salsa Latina (££)

Popular late-night haunt (open until 2AM) with a cocktail bar, terrace restaurant and live Brazilian-style music.

🖂 Rua Imperatriz Dona Amélia 101 ☎ 225 182 🕓 Lunch, dinner (high season only)

Vagrant (££)

Children will enjoy the novelty of eating on board ship in this 'floating' restaurant on the Funchal waterfront (but there is little risk of seasickness – this restaurant is now firmly bedded in concrete). The tall-masted schooner was formerly owned by the Beatles (one wonders whether they ever sailed in it), hence it is often referred to as the 'Beatles' Boat'. The menu ranges from pizzas and ice cream to typical Madeiran dishes.

🖂 Avenida das Comunidades Madeirenses ☎ 223 572
🕓 Lunch, dinner

Accompaniments

Any dish you order on Madeira is likely to be served with seasonal vegetables and salad. Chips are nearly always served as an accompaniment to meat dishes, and boiled potatoes with fish, unless you request otherwise. Banana fried in butter is an unusual but tasty accompaniment to many fish dishes, as is maize meal, formed into cubes and fried until the outside is crisp.

Western & Central Madeira

Madeiran Wine
As well as fortified Madeira wine, the island's vineyards produce a range of local red wines, which are drunk young, while they are still fresh, fruity and relatively low in alcohol. You may not find Madeiran wines on the wine list – restaurateurs prefer to sell more expensive imported wines with a higher mark-up – but you can try asking for local wine in snack bars and cafés.

Western Madeira

Água Mar (£)
With a terrace for fair-weather dining and a glassed-in dining room for when the sea spray gets too rough, this inexpensive restaurant serves standard Madeiran fare, including delicious roast chicken.

⊠ Ribeira Brava, on the seafront ☎ 951 148
🕐 Lunch, dinner. Closed Oct–Mar 🚌 4, 6, 7, 80, 107, 115, 127, 139, 142

Cachalote (££)
Enjoy fine views of the waves breaking against the rocky foreshore of Madeira's northern coast. The locally caught fish and seafood served here is as fresh as it can be.

⊠ Porto do Moniz, on the seafront ☎ 853 180
🕐 Lunch, dinner. Closed Oct–Mar 🚌 8, 139, 150

Fernandes (£)
Close to the Cachalote, this seasonal seafood restaurant is cheap, clean and friendly, which is why Portuguese holiday-makers flock here during the summer months.

⊠ Porto do Moniz, on north side of main square ☎ 853 147
🕐 Lunch, dinner. Closed Oct–Mar 🚌 8, 139, 150

Orca (££)
The fact that many coach parties stop off here for lunch on their round-the-island tours should not be taken as a sign that the food is inferior tourist fare. On the contrary, everything is fresh and well presented and the portions are large. Good views over the rock pools of Porto Moniz.

⊠ Porto do Moniz, on south side of main square ☎ 850 000
🕐 Lunch, dinner 🚌 8, 139, 150

Polo Norte (£)
The North Pole has a snack bar as well as a formal dining room, and is therefore a good choice if you just want a light meal or your children are hungry for a burger.

⊠ Porto do Moniz, on north side of main square ☎ 853 322
🕐 Lunch, dinner 🚌 8, 139, 150

Central Madeira

Aldeia do Monte (££)
The Aldeia do Monte restaurant commands sweeping views over Funchal and the harbour from its position in Monte village high above Madeira's capital. The restaurant features German, Portuguese and international dishes, with tables on the terrace for informal snacks and a rustic-style dining room inside.

⊠ Sitio do Pico, Monte
☎ 783 547 🕐 Lunch, dinner
🚌 Town bus 20, 21. Rural bus 103, 138

As Cabanas (££)
This restaurant, hotel and shopping complex, set down in the countryside between São Jorge and Arco de São Jorge, has African-style circular huts for rooms and a circular dining room. Keen prices and excellent Madeiran food make this a popular stopping-off point.

⊠ Cabanas ☎ 576 291
🕐 Lunch, dinner 🚌 103, 132, 138

Bodião (££)
Dine out on the slopes of Pico dos Barcelos, the volcanic peak just north of

Funchal's Hotel Zone, where the views, on a clear day, are everything you would expect from a terrace located 300m above sea level. *Bodião* (parrot fish) features as the speciality on a simple menu of grilled meats and fish.

📧 Caminho de São Martinho
☎ 263 078 🕐 Lunch, dinner
🚌 4, 6, 107, 154

Casa de Abrigo (££)

Sitting in woodland in the middle of the countryside, this roadside restaurant draws its trade from hungry walkers exploring the mountainous interior of the island, and from travellers passing between the north and south of the island. The welcoming old-fashioned interior is warmed by a wood fire (at this altitude the air has a chill even in summer) which is also used for cooking the traditional Madeiran meat-on-a-spit.

📧 Poiso, at the crossroads
☎ 782 269 🕐 Lunch, dinner
🚌 103, 132, 138

Encumeada Restaurant (££)

This roadside restaurant specialises in the kind of food that is rarely found elsewhere on the island – rabbit, suckling pig and hearty mountain beef and vegetable casseroles.

📧 2km south of Boca da Encumeada ☎ 952 319
🕐 Lunch, dinner 🚌 6, 139

O Colmo (££)

Santana's main restaurant inevitably attracts large tour groups, but the food is excellent, ranging from pizzas and well-filled sandwiches to grilled meats and fish.

📧 Santana, main street
☎ 573 666 🕐 Lunch, dinner
🚌 103, 132, 138

O Virgílio (£)

O Virgílio looks like a tourist trap, with its adjacent souvenir shop, but it retains the atmosphere of a good-value village bar, serving everything from a sandwich snack to a full meal of kebabs cooked over the log fire.

📧 São Vicente, on Porto Moniz road ☎ 842 467
🕐 Lunch, dinner 🚌 6, 132, 139, 150

Pousada do Pico do Arieiro (££)

The *pousada* (government-run hotel) on top of Madeira's third highest peak caters for hungry walkers in the café, with traditional Madeira fare, while the upmarket restaurant serves international-style food and offers fine views.

📧 Pico do Arieiro ☎ 230 110
🕐 Lunch, dinner

Quebra Mar (££)

The Quebra Mar is one of several restaurants in São Vicente serving standard Madeiran fare of kebabs and scabbard fish, plus grilled meats and fish.

📧 São Vicente, on the seafront
☎ 842 338 🕐 Lunch, dinner
🚌 6, 122, 139, 150

Quinta do Furão (££)

The Quinta do Furão is a working wine estate where visitors are encouraged to explore the vineyards, sample locally produced wines and eat either in the snack bar or the more upmarket restaurant.

📧 Achada do Gramacho, Santana ☎ 570 100 🕐 Lunch, dinner 🚌 103, 132, 138

Victor's Bar (££)

This popular roadside restaurant serves fresh trout from the adjacent trout farm. You can have trout in any form, from soup or smoked trout appetisers, to main courses of trout grilled, fried and poached.

📧 Ribeiro Frio, main street
☎ 575 898 🕐 Lunch, dinner
🚌 103, 138

A Feast of Fruit

Fruit lovers will be spoiled for choice on Madeira, where tropical bananas, mangoes, avocados, guavas, passion fruits, papaws, prickly pears and custard apples thrive on the sunny southern coastal strip, and the cooler mountain orchards produce cherries, pears, strawberries, walnuts and small but intensely flavoured apples. Because of Madeira's equitable climate, many of these fruits are in season all year round.

Eastern Madeira & Porto Santo

Madeiran Desserts
Although Madeirans have a sweet tooth, they do not normally eat puddings – desserts in most restaurants will be limited to a choice between fruit and several kinds of ice cream. When they want to indulge, Madeirans go to a *pastelaria*, a baker specialising in sweet pastries, most of which are based on nuts, dried fruit or egg custard.

Eastern Madeira

A Cornélia (£)
This is a simple roadside restaurant serving good home cooking to hungry travellers at reasonable prices. A Cornélia is located just south of Camacha.

⊠ **Vale do Paraiso, Camacha**
☎ **792 892** ⊙ **Lunch, dinner**
🚌 **29, 77**

Casa Velha do Palheiro (£££)
Outside of Funchal's five-star hotels, it is unusual to find cooking of gourmet-standard on Madeira. This elegant restaurant, in a converted mansion on the edge of the Quinta do Palheiro estate, is a rare exception: the stylish dishes served here combine the best of Madeira's fresh ingredients with ideas borrowed from Italy, the Mediterranean and the Far East.

⊠ **Estalagem Casa Velha do Palheiro** ☎ **794 901** ⊙ **Lunch, dinner. Booking advised**
🚌 **Town buses 29, 36, 37**

Inn and Art (££)
This friendly cliff-top establishment in Caniço de Baixa combines a restaurant, wine bar, café and hotel with a gallery of original paintings by contemporary artists from all over the world, many of which are for sale. Good range of wines.

⊠ **Caniço de Baixo R61/R62**
☎ **938 200** ⊙ **Lunch, dinner**
🚌 **2, 113, 114, 155**

Mercado Velho (££)
Machico's Old Market makes an atmospheric base for this pleasant restaurant with its tree-shaded terrace and fountain.

⊠ **Rua do Mercado, Machico**
☎ **965 926** ⊙ **Lunch, dinner**
🚌 **20, 23, 53, 78, 113, 156**

O Facho (££)
A lively restaurant which is popular with locals. The snack bar is ideal for simple eats, or for a more formal occasion, try the dining room next door.

⊠ **Praça do Salazar, Machico**
☎ **962 786** ⊙ **Lunch, dinner**
🚌 **20, 23, 53, 78, 113, 156**

Pastelaria Galã (£)
Pop in here for a mid-morning snack or afternoon tea and sample the delights of Madeiran cakes, made with eggs, almonds, fruits and nuts. The small restaurant also serves snacks and sandwiches.

⊠ **Rua da Mercado, Machico**
☎ **965 720** ⊙ **Lunch, dinner**
🚌 **20, 23, 53, 78, 113, 156**

La Perla Gourmet Restaurant (£££)
Set in beautifully gardened grounds, La Perla occupies a typical Madeiran *quinta*, a manor house once at the centre of a wine estate, now converted to provide a stylish restaurant. The Italian-influenced menu includes wild mushroom dishes, veal and zabaglione, as well as grilled fish and, in tribute to Madeira's volcanic origins, beef served sizzling on a heated volcanic stone.

⊠ **Quinta Splendida, Sítio da Vargem, Caniço** ☎ **930 400**
⊙ **Lunch, dinner** 🚌 **2, 113, 114, 155**

La Terraça (££)
This restaurant with its outdoor terrace setting is

ideal for long lazy lunches, or dinner in the balmy evening air, while enjoying the valley views down to the sea. Fish is the speciality.

✉ **Sitio da Vargem, Caniço** ☎ **933 898** ◷ **Lunch, dinner** 🚌 **2, 113, 114, 155**

Village Pub (£)

This English-run bar and restaurant is popular for its true pub atmosphere. The speciality is Full English Breakfast (served throughout opening hours). There is a good choice of beers, and bar snacks are available.

✉ **Caniço, town centre** ☎ **932 596** ◷ **Noon–2AM. Closed Mon** 🚌 **2, 113, 114, 155**

Vista Mar (££)

You can sample typical Portuguese cuisine, with different daily specials, at this popular seafront restaurant, five minutes' walk from the Dom Pedro Hotel in Garajau.

✉ **Garajau** ☎ **934 110** ◷ **Lunch, dinner** 🚌 **2, 113, 114, 155**

Porto Santo

Bar Torres (£)

Roast chicken as you probably haven't tasted it for a long time draws appreciative crowds to this bar with its vine-covered dining terrace; on the road to Fonte da Areia.

✉ **Camacha** ☎ **984 373** ◷ **Lunch, dinner; booking essential in high season**

Estrela do Norte (£)

If the Bar Torres (➤ above) is full, this neighbouring restaurant is a good alternative.

✉ **Camacha** ☎ **983 400** ◷ **Lunch, dinner; booking essential in high season**

Mar e Sol (££)

This deservedly popular restaurant stands alongside Porto Santo's glorious beach, midway between Vila Baleira and Ponta da Calheta. The main items on the menu are fresh fish and seafood.

✉ **Campo de Baixo** ☎ **982 269** ◷ **Lunch, dinner**

O Forno (££)

A variation on the usual theme of *espetada* kebabs is the house speciality, *picado*, consisting of small chunks of beef spiced up with garlic and chilli. The excellent home-baked bread is cooked in the wood-fired oven that gives the restaurant its name.

✉ **Rampa da Fontinha, Vila Baleira** ☎ **985 141** ◷ **Lunch, dinner**

Pôr-do-Sol (£££)

This smart daytime café and night-time restaurant serves wonderful grilled fish but is best known for its views of the setting sun from Porto Santo's southernmost tip.

✉ **Calheta** ☎ **984 380** ◷ **Lunch, dinner**

Teodorico (£)

This small restaurant, which opens only for the summer months, specialises in beef kebabs which are cooked as authentically as you are likely to find anywhere on Madeira.

✉ **Serra da Fora** ☎ **982 257** ◷ **Lunch, dinner. Closed Oct–Apr**

Liqueurs

Madeirans have a gift for turning even the most unlikely ingredients into alcoholic liqueurs. As you tour the island you will be offered local specialities, such as the delicious *ginga*, made from cherries, *castanha*, produced from sweet chestnuts, and *maracujá*, made from passion fruit. Liqueurs are also made from fennel (*funcho*), almonds (*amêndo*), walnuts (*noz*) and banana (*banau*). Less palatable to many, but a powerful cold remedy, is the menthol-flavoured *eucolipto* liqueur made from the seeds of the island's ubiquitous eucalyptus trees.

Funchal

Prices

Prices are for a double room, including breakfast and tax:

£ = under 50 euros
££ = 50–100 euros
£££ = over 100 euros

The prices for rooms in the more expensive hotels are often cheaper if booked as part of a package holiday. Conversely, the tour companies often charge more for the cheaper hotels than you could get by booking direct. Nearly all hotels on Madeira include breakfast as part of the room price. Half- and full-board terms are also available at the more expensive hotels.

Carlton Park Hotel (£££)

The Carlton Park is the closest of Madeira's five-star hotels to the centre of Funchal; from here it is a short stroll through the Jardim de Santa Catarina to the downtown area. This is also Madeira's liveliest hotel for nightlife, with a top-class cabaret programme (➤ 114), regular discos and a casino on the grounds. The architecture was adventurous in its day: designed in the 1970s by Oscar Niemeyer, the Brazilian architect, the hotel follows Corbusian principles in being built on stilts to allow uninterrupted views across the hotel gardens to the sea. The circular casino in the grounds is identical to one by the same architect built in the Chinese-Portuguese colony of Macau, and is known locally (and perhaps disparagingly) as the 'rack of lamb'. Rooms are large and well equipped and there are good swimming and tennis facilities in the grounds.

✉ **Rua Imperatriz Dona Amélia** ☎ **209 100** 🕒 **All year**

Castanheiro Apartamentos (££)

This apartment hotel offers bright, well-furnished rooms, all equipped with air-conditioning, television and CD player, plus a small kitchenette and dining area right in the heart of Funchal. The hotel is opposite the newly created University of Madeira, which occupies the former Jesuit seminary, just north of the Praça do Município – during the day the street bustles with students coming and going, but there is little traffic after

dark. Facilities include a restaurant, snack bar and private parking.

✉ **Rua do Castanheiro 27** ☎ **227 060** 🕒 **All year**

Cliff Bay (£££)

The Cliff Bay Resort Hotel is just around the corner from Reid's and enjoys similar panoramic views over Funchal and the harbour. Being new it has several innovative features, including rooms designed especially for visitors with disabilities. There is a large outdoor pool in the grounds and an indoor heated pool, plus health club, tennis and squash courts, gym and sauna.

✉ **Estrada Monumental 147** ☎ **707 700** 🕒 **All year**

D'Ajuda (££)

This hotel and apartment complex, 3.5km from the centre of Funchal, is ideal for people who want to combine the freedom of self-catering with the facilities of a four-star hotel. Choose between twin-bedded hotel rooms with balconies, studio apartments for 2–3 people with kitchenettes, or 4-bed apartments. Facilities include outdoor and indoor pools, and free transport into central Funchal by courtesy bus.

✉ **Caminho Velha da Ajuda, São Martinho** ☎ **761 316** 🕒 **All year**

Eden Mar (££)

Excellent value aparthotel close to the supermarkets and the Lido complex in the Hotel Zone. The studios and suites all have a kitchenette with fridge and two cooking rings. Facilities on site include a swimming pool,

gym, sauna, Jacuzzi and tennis courts.

✉ **Rua do Gorgulho 2** ☎ **709 700** 🕒 **All year**

Estrelicia (££)

The Hotel Estrelicia forms part of a complex with two other hotels, set in a quiet area of the Hotel Zone, sharing facilities such as heated swimming pools, restaurants, tennis courts and gym. There is also a regular minibus service into Funchal. In the same complex is the Mimosa Aparthotel (☎ 765 021), whose rooms have sink, fridge and cooking rings for self-catering. The complex prides itself on an active entertainments programme, with magic shows for children, folklore evenings, and regular quiz and competition nights.

✉ **Caminho Velha do Ajuda** ☎ **706 600** 🕒 **All year**

Madeira (££)

This small hotel opposite the Scottish Church and looking out over the Jardim de São Francisco public gardens could not be more central, but being one block back from Funchal's main street, it remains a peaceful spot. Comfortably furnished rooms, friendly service and a small roof-top pool.

✉ **Rua Ivens 21** ☎ **230 071** 🕒 **All year**

Carlton Madeira (£££)

Along with the Savoy and the Carlton Park, the Carlton Madeira enjoys a location close to downtown Funchal. The hotel is in two parts; rooms in the 16-storey main block enjoy fine views to the harbour or to the mountains, while the pool terrace block has rooms looking over the hotel's two large swimming pools. Other facilities include a paddling pool, tennis courts, mini golf, a gym and a sauna. For children, there is a play area, and a Kids' Activity Club operates during the summer.

✉ **Largo António Nobre** ☎ **239 500** 🕒 **All year**

Madeira Palácio (£££)

Being on the fringes of Funchal (5km from the city centre), the Madeira Palácio is less expensive than rival five-star hotels, and is a good choice if you want luxury in peaceful surroundings at bargain prices. Instead of views over Funchal, rooms look towards the towering cliffs of Cabo Girão. A courtesy bus provides a regular service into Funchal, but many visitors prefer just to stay in the hotel, enjoying the pool, gardens, tennis courts, games room and sauna, plus nightly live music and regular folklore evenings.

✉ **Estrada Monumental 265** ☎ **702 702** 🕒 **All year**

Monte Carlo (££)

The steep walk up to this hotel is rewarded by the views to be had across the red-tiled roofs of Funchal from the terrace and from many rooms. The oldest part of the hotel consists of an elegant 19th-century mansion, and the modern rooms are built in traditional Madeiran style. Facilities include a restaurant, bar and a mini-bus service into town.

✉ **Calçada da Saúde 10** ☎ **226 131** 🕒 **All year**

A Room with a View

Hotels charge up to 20 per cent extra for a room with a sea view. You may consider this worth while if the alternative is a room on the street side of the hotel, for many rooms in the Hotel Zone look out on to the busy Estrada Monumental. Having said that, the road is only busy during the day, and the opening of the new express road to the north of Funchal has diverted most of the through-traffic away from the city.

Location, Location

Hotels on Madeira tend to be priced according to location: the closer to the city centre, the higher the price. To be really central, opt for the Savoy or Carlton Park. Reid's is, despite its luxurious ambience, some 30 minutes' walk from the centre, and most of the hotels in the Hotel Zone are further out still. Those some way from the town centre are often the cheapest, however, and they represent a good bargain since many provide a courtesy bus into town.

Self-catering

For visitors with families, the option of self-catering may appeal if you want to make your own meals for the children. Ask your travel agent about the availability of aparthotels, where the accommodation includes a small kitchen and a living room.

Porto Santa Maria (£££)

This brand new hotel in the Zona Velha, or Old Town, brings four-star luxury to a part of Funchal that has only had cheap and old-fashioned accommodation up to now. The hotel is perfectly located for visitors who want to be right where the action is, without sacrificing the facilities of an upmarket hotel. The hotel is fronted by a sun terrace with outdoor pool and bar, and some of Funchal's best restaurants are literally on the doorstep.

✉ **Avenida do Mar** ☎ **206 700** 🕐 **All year**

Quinta da Bela Vista (££)

Although you need a car to reach this elegant mansion hotel (located some 15 minutes from the centre) the price is worth paying for stylishly furnished rooms, many with antiques, and polished service.

✉ **Caminho Avista Navios 4** ☎ **706 400** 🕐 **All year**

Quinta da Penha de França (££)

Many *quintas* (aristocratic mansions, often with extensive gardens and land holdings) were swept away when Funchal's Hotel Zone was created in the 1980s, but this fine building managed to survive in a prime spot behind the Casino Palace Hotel. Now converted to a fine hotel itself, the Quinta is a place of old-fashioned elegance combined with all mod cons.

✉ **Rua Penha de França 2** ☎ **204 650** 🕐 **All year**

Quinta do Sol (££)

This friendly hotel overlooks the gardens of the Quinta do Magnólia park, with its tennis and squash courts (► 113), which guests can use for a small charge. In addition, the hotel has its own heated swimming pool and games room. For an added touch of luxury, go for rooms in the new wing. The hotel puts on a weekly folklore show, plus live music most nights in the cocktail bar.

✉ **Rua Dr Pita 6** ☎ **764 151** 🕐 **All year**

Quinta Perestrelo (££)

This small 19th-century mansion has rooms overlooking the extensive public gardens of the nearby Quinta do Magnólia. Friendly service.

✉ **Rua do Dr Pita 3** ☎ **763 720** 🕐 **All year**

Reid's Palace (£££)

Reid's is one of the world's best-known and prestigious hotels, gaining its name for quiet sophistication in the days when the rich and leisured classes would spend the winter on Madeira to escape the cold of northern Europe. William Reid, the founder, one of 12 sons of an impoverished Scottish crofter, worked his passage to Madeira in 1836 and set up a rental agency. Wealthy visitors would rely on Reid to find and furnish them a suitable mansion or villa for the duration of their stay, paying him handsomely to do so. With the money he made, he bought the cliff-top site of Reid's Hotel, with its uninterrupted sea views and immaculate gardens. Reid died in 1888 before seeing his dream hotel completed: it opened in 1891, and has numbered royalty, film stars and heads of state among its guests ever since. For some, this elegant, understated hotel will be far too formal (though not compulsory, most guests wear evening dress for dinner); for others it will be a welcome escape from the bustling world.

✉ **Estrada Monumental 139**
☎ **717 171** 🕐 **All year**

Residencial Gordon (£)

Caught in a time warp, the Gordon is a quiet, old-fashioned hotel, furnished in a style that remains popular on Madeira but which went out of fashion elsewhere in the 1950s. Some rooms overlook the pretty gardens of the English Church (whose Library is open to visitors; the coffee mornings that take place here after the Sunday morning service also provide a popular meeting point for visitors and long-stay Madeira residents).

✉ **Rua do Quebra Costas 34**
☎ **742 366** 🕐 **All year**

Residencial Santa Clara (£)

The Santa Clara hotel offers budget accommodation in a gracious and dignified old building with grand interiors; the catch is that it is a stiff uphill walk from the centre of Funchal, past the Santa Clara Convent, so you need to be fit to get here.

✉ **Calçada do Pico 16B**
☎ **742 194** 🕐 **All year**

Savoy (£££)

One of Madeira's longest-established luxury hotels, the Savoy is quiet and dignified but also caters well for families, with friendly staff and an excellent range of sports facilities. Swimmers have a choice of four pools, including the luxurious facilities of the newly opened tropical lido. In addition, there are tennis courts, a games room and a health centre, plus a library for those who prefer less strenuous activities. Rooms are large and the hotel is a 15-minute stroll from downtown Funchal.

✉ **Avenida do Infante**
☎ **222 031** 🕐 **All year**

Sirius (£)

Comfortable rooms at reasonable prices in a bustling street in the heart of Funchal.

✉ **Rua das Hortas 31–7**
☎ **226 117** 🕐 **All year**

Vila Ramos (££)

Enjoy all the facilities of the Savoy Hotel without paying luxury hotel prices. The Vila Ramos is under the same management as the Savoy, and guests can use that hotel's facilities. The hotel is in a quiet location, about 15 minutes from the shops and restaurants of the Lido area, and with a regular mini-bus service to downtown Funchal. Rooms are larger than average, with balconies.

✉ **Azinhaga da Casa Branca 7**
☎ **706 280** 🕐 **All year**

Windsor (£)

This friendly modern hotel is buried in the heart of the maze of lanes near the Carmo church in central Funchal. Most rooms face into an inner courtyard, rather than the street, so noise is not a problem. There is a tiny roof-top pool, and ample parking in the hotel garage.

✉ **Rua das Hortas 4C**
☎ **233081** 🕐 **All year**

High and Low Season Prices

Hotel prices on Madeira reflect the demand at different times of year. Late July and all of August is expensive because Portuguese holiday-makers come to the island to escape the heat of the mainland. The two weeks of Christmas and New Year cost even more because many people come for the illuminations and the spectacular New Year fireworks: hotels not only charge extra at this time of year, they also add in the cost of compulsory dinner dance tickets for Christmas Eve, Christmas Day and New Year's Eve. By contrast, January, February, March and November are low season months when some real bargains can be had, even at such prestigious hotels as Reid's.

Madeira & Porto Santo

Quintas, Estalagems and Residencials

Rural hotels on Madeira go by a variety of different names, but usually any establishment that calls itself an *estalagem* or a *residencial* is a small hotel, with perhaps 30 or so rooms, that prides itself on a certain character. Many are conversions of rural mansions, as are *quintas* – *quinta* being the Portuguese word for a manor house at the centre of a wine or agricultural estate.

Western Madeira

Jardim do Atlantico (£££)

One of the few luxury hotels located in the western part of Madeira, the Jardim do Atlantico promotes itself as a health resort, with a range of programmes to help you get fit. Not all the treatments on offer involve strenuous exercise or rigorous dieting: yoga, meditation, massage, hydrotherapy and acupuncture are all available, as well as fitness classes and countryside walks. Vegetarian dishes feature on the restaurant menu.

✉ **Lomba da Rocha, Prazeres, Calheta** ☎ **822 200**
🕐 **All year**

Residencial Orca (££)

This small 12-room hotel is perched above the rock pools at Porto do Moniz on the northwesternmost tip of Madeira. Thanks to its popularity with round-the-island travellers, this is now a surprisingly busy and cosmopolitan spot.

✉ **Sitio das Poças, Porto do Moniz** ☎ **850 000** 🕐 **All year**

Central Madeira

Cabanas de São Jorge (££)

Guests at the Cabanas de São Jorge holiday village stay in round huts inspired by Zulu architecture (the owner spent many years in South Africa). The huts are set among pine and eucalyptus trees, and there are fine views from the carefully tended gardens over the cliffs of Madeira's north coast.

✉ **Beira da Quinta, São Jorge** ☎ **576 291** 🕐 **All year**

Estalagem do Mar (££)

Built in a crescent shape on the very edge of the sea, the modern Estalagem do Mar has rooms that look out over the circular outdoor pool to the rocky foreshore. Facilities include an indoor heated pool, a games room, a sauna and a gym.

✉ **Sao Viçente** ☎ **840 010**
🕐 **All year**

Pousada do Pico do Arieiro (££)

Perched high above the clouds, on top of Pico do Arieiro, at a height of 1,818m above sea level, this state-run hotel enjoys stunning views of the volcanic landscapes and knife-edge ridges making up Madeira's central mountain range. Visitors come here to get an early start on their hiking trips to Pico Ruivo, or to watch the spectacular effects created by the rising and setting sun, or to enjoy the clarity and detail of the night sky. Rooms have terraces and balconies for enjoying the view, plus all mod cons, including satellite television.

✉ **Pico do Arieiro** ☎ **230 110**
🕐 **All year; book well in advance**

Pousada dos Vinháticos (££)

This charming *pousada* caters for walkers exploring the unspoiled woodland terrain in the spectacular Serra da Água Valley, south of the Encumeada pass. Facilities are simple but adequate.

✉ **Serra da Água** ☎ **952 344**
🕐 **All year; book in advance**

Eastern Madeira

Estalagem Relógio (£)
Good value accommodation in the 'wicker' village of Camacha, with spectacular views from some rooms. The nearby restaurant has regular Madeiran song and dance shows by one of the island's best troupes.
🖂 Sítio da Igreja, Camacha
☎ 922 777 🕒 All year

Estalagem do Santo (££)
Popular with golfers, the Estalagem do Santo is a short drive away from the Santo da Serra golf course. Set among woodland, with manicured grounds and a new indoor swimming pool , the hotel has modern rooms built around the core of a 200 year old mansion.
🖂 Santo António da Serra
☎ 552 595 🕒 All year

Quinta Splendida (£££)
The old pink-walled *quinta* now houses the excellent restaurant; the modern guest rooms are set around a courtyard, surrounded by tropical gardens.
🖂 Sítio de Vargem, Caniço
☎ 930 400 🕒 All year

Residencial Machico (£)
Right in the heart of Machico and a good choice for budget travellers, with private bathrooms and plenty of restaurants nearby.
🖂 Praça Salazar, Machico
☎ 965 575 🕒 All year

Roca Mar (£££)
The Roca Mar enjoys a spectacular location on the cliff tops south of Caniço. The rocky cove at the foot of the cliffs has been converted into a lido, with swimming pools, sun terraces, and a pier for access to the sheltered blue waters just offshore. There is a well established diving club based at the hotel offering lessons and accompanied dives, plus a full range of evening entertainments and a regular shuttle bus service to Funchal.
🖂 Caniço de Baixa
☎ 934 334 🕒 All year

Royal Orchid (££)
This aparthotel complex, alongside the Roca Mar, has modern facilities, including indoor and outdoor pools, a Jacuzzi, a Turkish steam room and sauna, gym and games rooms. The apartments are built in terraced blocks with sea views, each studio has its own fully equipped kitchenette
🖂 Caniço de Baixo
☎ 934 600 🕒 All year

Porto Santo

Luamar (££)
Built right among the sand dunes of Port Santo's beach; rooms have kitchenettes and there is a small supermarket on site. A shuttle bus runs to Vila Baleira.
🖂 Sítio de Cabeço de Ponta
☎ 984 121 🕒 May–Oct only

Porto Santo (£££)
The beautiful gardens of this hotel merge imperceptibly with Porto Santo's golden beach. There are windsurfing boards and bicycles available, plus a mini golf course and tennis courts.
🖂 Ribeiro Cochino, Campo de Baixo ☎ 982 381 🕒 May–Oct only

Pousadas
Pousadas are a unique Portuguese institution – a chain of state-run inns set in scenic locations, often in important historic buildings. The two on Madeira are relatively modern and purpose-built, but they occupy prime spots: one on the peak of Madeira's third highest mountain, the Pico do Arieiro, and the other on the edge of a protected area of virgin forest at the centre of the island.

Shopping Centres and Markets

Places to Shop

All the shops mentioned in this section are to be found in Funchal, unless otherwise stated.

Shopping Centres

The late 1990s saw a rash of new shopping malls being built in Funchal. The biggest (with a huge supermarket in the basement) is the Anadia Shopping Centre, located directly opposite the Mercado dos Lavradores (the Workers' Market) on Rua Dr Fernão Omelas. The smartest, with upmarket boutiques and furnishing stores, is the Galerias São Lourenço, opposite the tourist office on Avenida Arriaga.

Bazar Oliveiras

Everything from honey cake (*bolo de mel*) to videos of Madeira, and from tacky keyrings to sophisticated handmade embroidery, is for sale here under one roof.

✉ **Rua das Murcas 6**
☎ **224 632** ⏰ **Daily 10–7**

Casa do Turista

The Casa do Turista offers a comprehensive selection of Madeiran and Portuguese products under one roof. The shop occupies an elegant townhouse in the centre of Funchal, and products such as lace, embroidery and other textiles, pottery, glass, embroidery and furniture are displayed beneath ornate plastered ceilings, and fine paintings are displayed on the walls. You can browse for anything from a wicker cache pot to a complete dinner service.

✉ **Rua do Conselheiro José Silvestre Ribeiro 2** ☎ **224 907**
⏰ **Mon–Fri 10–7, Sat 10–1**

Eden Mar Shopping Centre

Situated right in the heart of the Hotel Zone, this modern shopping centre, which includes a supermarket, clothing shops, banks, art gallery and wine shops, is the place where most visitors to the island come to do their shopping.

✉ **Rua do Gorgulho** ☎ **No telephone** ⏰ **Daily 10–7**

Marina Shopping Centre

Three floors of shops, from electrical goods and clothing to beachwear and disco gear. Look out for fine leather goods at Sacco et Compa in the basement, and for men's clothes at Wesley, on street level.

✉ **Avenida Arriaga (the end nearest the Hotel Zone)**
⏰ **Mon–Fri 10–7, Sat 10–1 (with some shops staying open all day Sat & Sun)**

Markets

Although supermarkets exist on Madeira, many people still shop for daily necessities in the local covered market. There is a huge market in Funchal (► 20) which operates all day, every day except Sunday. Elsewhere the markets are much smaller and are usually closed by lunchtime – for the best choice you need to arrive before 9:30. Markets are usually divided into two areas, with fish being sold from great white marble slabs in one half, and fruits and vegetables artfully displayed in the other half. Meat and delicatessen goods are sold from enclosed shops around the market perimeter.

Markets, open from 8 to 1 Monday to Friday, are to be found in all the main towns:

Ribeira Brava: next to bus station, on seafront road.
Calheta: on seafront road.
Câmara de Lobos: on the road that skirts the western side of the harbour.
Santa Cruz: to the west of the Palm Beach lido on the seafront esplanade.
Machico: on the eastern side of the fortress that houses the Tourist Office on the seafront road.

In addition, Curral das Freiras hosts a general market in the main street on Sunday mornings where a wide range of clothing and household goods, as well as edible produce, is sold.

Books and Home Furnishings

Bookshops

Livraria Pátio
If you are desperate for reading material on Madeira, your best hope is the Pátio Bookshop, housed in several separate shops around the very attractive O Pátio café (➤ 44). Owned by John and Susan Farrow, who also run the English School on Madeira, the shop has a comprehensive selection of guide books to the island, plus a fascinating range of antiquarian books and best-selling fiction titles in English, French, German and Portuguese. The shop also stocks a wide range of artists' materials.

✉ Rua da Carreira 43 ☎ 224 490 ⏲ Mon–Fri 10–7, Sat 10–1

Collectables

The Collectors Shop
Old postcards of Madeira make an unusual souvenir; browse for postcards, greetings cards, postage stamps, coins and banknotes, medallions and old book covers, as well as minerals and precious stones at this collectors' cornucopia.

✉ Avenida Arriaga 75 ☎ 223 070 ⏲ Mon–Fri 10–7, Sat 10–1

Furnishings

Carpetland
Large stocks of oriental rugs can be viewed at this store.

✉ Rua das Murcas 16–18 ☎ 223 522 ⏲ Mon–Fri 10–7, Sat 10–1

Cayres
A good selection of modern Portuguese ceramics.

✉ Rua Dr Fernão Ornelas 56A/B ☎ 226 104 ⏲ Mon–Fri 10–7, Sat 10–11

Housekeeper
Fabrics, lighting and decorative products.

✉ Rua dos Arahhas ☎ 228999 ⏲ Mon–Fri 10–7, Sat 10–1

Intemporâneo Interiores
Modern furniture, lighting and furnishing fabrics.

✉ Rua das Netos 18 ☎ 238 076 ⏲ Mon–Fri 10–1, 3–7, Sat 10–1

O Imaginário
Picture frames, ceramics, fabrics and silk flowers, plus a good choice of Portuguese Christmas crib figures and tree decorations.

✉ Rua das Aranhas 34 ☎ 230 307 ⏲ Mon–Fri 10–7, Sat 10–1

Tela
Boxes made of silver and carved wood, seashells, bird cages – attractive souvenirs.

✉ Rua da Carreira 174 ☎ 230 240 ⏲ Mon–Fri 10–7, Sat 10–1

Tapestry

The Kiekeben Shop
Finished wall hangings, chair covers, carpets and even luggage and handbags made from tapestry.

✉ Rua da Carreira 194 ☎ 222 073 ⏲ Mon–Fri 10–7, Sat 10–1

Madeira Sun
Do-it-yourself tapestry kits at a fraction of the price you would pay for the finished articles.

✉ Avenida Zarco 4 ⏲ Mon–Fri 10–7, Sat 10–1

Tapestry
Herbert Kiekeben, a German artist, introduced the craft of sewing pictures on canvas to Madeira in 1938. Though it has not outgrown embroidery in the Madeiran craft league, locally made products now sell worldwide.

Arts and Crafts

Madeiran Embroidery

The art of fine embroidery was introduced to Madeira by Elizabeth Phelps, the daughter of an English wine merchant, in the 1850s. This was a time of great calamity on Madeira, with disease having decimated the island's wine crops and cholera raging through the population (7,000 people died in 1852 alone). The resulting poverty so distressed Miss Phelps that she established her embroidery business as a means of supplementing the islanders' meagre incomes. Today, 20,000 Madeirans are involved in the business, including men and boys.

Knitwear

Knitted cotton sweaters and thick Madeiran hats with ear flaps are sold by roadside stall-holders all over Madeira. Though not always in fashionable colours or designs, they are, nevertheless, a bargain.

Embroidery

Madeiran embroidery is made by hand and it takes many hours to produce even a simple napkin – hence the high prices charged for a blouse, nightdress or tablecloth. True Madeiran lace is distinguished from machine-made products (mostly imported from the Far East) by the special lead seal that is attached to each piece after it has been inspected for quality and finish. The seal (which is slowly being replaced by a similarly shaped hologram) is a guarantee of authenticity granted by IBTAM (➤ 34), the island's handicrafts institute.

Funchal has many embroidery 'factories' where the designs are pricked out on to fine linen cloth before it is sent to outworkers to be embroidered. Here the finished articles are washed, ironed and inspected before being given their mark of authenticity. It is well worth visiting a factory to learn about the process before you make your final purchase.

Casa Regional

This store features fine embroidery and a range of Madeiran souvenirs.
✉ Avenida Zarco 15
☎ 224 943 🕐 Mon–Fri 10–7, Sat 10–1

Patricio & Gouveia

This is one of the best and biggest factories in Madeira, with a large selection of garments and table linen.
✉ Rua do Visconde de Anadia 33 ☎ 220 801 🕐 Mon–Fri 10–7, Sat 10–1

Leatherwork

Portuguese craftsmanship in leather is renowned throughout Europe. Madeira has a number of shops selling beautifully made goods that cost about half the price they would fetch in Paris, London or Rome.

Artecouro

This shop specialises in beautiful leather goods produced by local craftsmen (you can visit the factory where they are made, at Rua Carlos Azevedo Menezes 16).
✉ Rua da Alfândega 15
☎ 237 256 🕐 Mon–Fri 10–7, Sat 10–1

Gonçalves & Silva

For a fine pair of traditional Madeiran leather ankle boots, with turned down tops, visit this workshop in the Zona Velha (Old Town) and watch them being made before you buy.
✉ Rua da Portão de São Tiaga 22 ☎ 934 663 🕐 Mon–Fri 10–7, Sat 10–1

Safa Pele

This shop has a good choice of elegant leather handbags, wallets, briefcases and luggage.
✉ Rua das Murcas 26A
☎ 223 619 🕐 Daily 10–7

Wickerwork

For the best selection of wickerwork, visit the Café Relógio in Camacha (➤ 76).

Sousa & Gonçalves

Here you will find willow furniture and basket-work at factory prices. Large items can be shipped.
✉ Rua do Castanheiro 47
☎ 223 626 🕐 Daily 10–7

Flowers and Wine

Flowers

You can buy flowers in the market or from stallholders around the cathedral square in Funchal, but the advantage of buying from shops is that they will pack your purchases in special protective boxes so that they will withstand the journey home.

A Rosa

Order your flowers two or three days before your departure and they will be delivered to your hotel fresh on the day you leave.

✉ **Rua Imperatriz Dona Amélia 126** ☎ **764 111** 🕐 **Mon–Fri 10–7, Sat 10–1**

Boa Vista Orchids

Whether you want to buy orchids or not, it is worth visiting Boa Vista Orchids just for the lovely subtropical gardens that surround the Quinta da Boa Vista (the well-named Good View Mansion).

✉ **Rua Lombo da Boa Vista** ☎ **220 468** 🕐 **Mon–Sat 9–5:30**

Gardenia Azul

Outside the Savoy Hotel and convenient for the Hotel Zone.

✉ **Avenida do Infante** ☎ **234 171** 🕐 **Mon–Fri 10–7, Sat 10–1**

Jardim Orquídea

The Orchid Garden is a working nursery with some 4,000 different varieties of tropical orchid on display (flowering all year – main season November to February). You can visit the breeding laboratories and buy *in vitro* plants, grown in gel in a plastic tube to take home (EU customs regulations allow the importation of plants so long as there is no soil with them). Entrance charge.

✉ **Rua Pita da Silva 37** ☎ **238 444** 🕐 **Daily 9–8**

Magnolia Flower Shop

Excellent selection of cut and dried flowers, plus pot plants, bulbs and orchids.

✉ **Loja 1, Casino Park Hotel Gardens** ☎ **222 577** 🕐 **Daily 10–7**

Wine & Liqueurs

The most enjoyable way to buy your wine is to visit a wine lodge, where you can sample the products. For an introduction to the history of Madeira, take a tour of the Adegas de São Francisco wine lodge (➤ 18).

Artur de Barros e Sousa

Visitors are greeted by the warm evocative smells of old wood and rich wine at this old cobbled-floor wine lodge.

✉ **Rua dos Ferreiros 109** ☎ **220 622** 🕐 **Mon–Fri 10–7, Sat 10–1**

Diogos Wine Shop

Not only a comprehensive stock of Madeiran and Portuguese wines, but also a Columbus Museum alongside.

✉ **Avenida Arriaga 48** ☎ **233 357** 🕐 **Daily 10–7**

D'Oliveiras

A traditional wine lodge with free tastings.

✉ **Rua dos Ferreiros 107** ☎ **220 784** 🕐 **Mon–Fri 10–7, Sat 10–1**

Henriques & Henriques

Another long-established wine lodge.

✉ **Sítio de Belém, Câmara de Lobos** ☎ **941 551** 🕐 **Mon–Fri 10–7, Sat 10–1**

Dancers on a Stick

Among Madeiran souvenirs, look out for the percussive musical instrument called *brinquinhos*. These consist of a number of dolls in Madeiran costume, holding cymbals and bells, which clap their hands as you move them up and down a central stick.

Children's Attractions

Indulgence

The Portuguese love children, especially babies and toddlers. Do not be surprised or offended if strangers touch your children as they pass – fair-haired children in particular are regarded as fortunate, so yours will be patted on the head or shoulders for luck and as an expression of approval. In restaurants, children are welcomed and indulged, and parents can bask in the extra attention that (well-behaved) families get wherever they go.

Madeira has few genuinely child-friendly attractions, so you may need to exercise some imagination to keep your young ones amused. The top attraction in Funchal is the aquarium in the Museu Municipal (▶ 41).

Younger children will enjoy the small playground and aviary in the Jardim de Santa Catarina (▶ 36), and the antics of the tropical birds in the Jardim dos Loiros (▶ 36).

Boat Trips

Head for Funchal's yachting marina to see the range of boat trips on offer. Most operators use motor-powered boats, but you can also book excursions on the yacht *Albatroz*, a fully licensed 20m yacht built in 1939, available for hire with crew for parties of up to 20 people. Unless they are prone to seasickness, most children love this experience of travelling at speed under sail. Trips can be booked through any travel agency, through the tourist office in Funchal or through Turispeca (☎ 231 063) or Costa do Sol (☎ 238 538).

Another child-pleasing alternative is the Santa Maria, a full-size replica of Columbus's ship, which sails twice daily, weather permitting (☎ 220 327).

Dolphin-watching

Ecologically minded teenagers will love this trip, provided that they are aware that sighting dolphins is not guaranteed – even so, the boat operators who lead these trips usually know

where to look. Two-hour trips take place every Wednesday, departing from Funchal at 10, 1 and 4. Further details from Albatroz Dolphin Watch, Funchal Marina (☎ 223 366).

Football

The stadium to the north of the Hotel Zone is home to Madeira's first division football team, C S Marítimo. Football-mad teenagers will find that the games here are friendly and are not marred by any of the crowd violence that can spoil enjoyment of the game elsewhere. Home matches are played on alternate Sunday afternoons in the season.

✉ **Estádio dos Barreiros**
☎ **Tourist office 225 658**

Grutas de São Vicente

The top attraction for children on Madeira is the newly opened cave system just north of São Vicentes. The only drawback is that the guided tour is so short – you spend only 15–20 minutes inside the caves. Children do go free, however.

The caves are unusual in being created not by water erosion, but by molten lava, flowing down from the volcanic peaks of the Paúl da Serra, when they last erupted 400,000 years ago. The lava flowed into joints in the rock, melting a tubular path, which visitors now walk along. What appear to be stalactites hanging from the ceiling are drips of molten rock, frozen *in situ*. The lava flows themselves look just like molten

chocolate, complete with ripples, but hardened into solid rock.

A small museum on the site is devoted to explaining the flora and fauna of the Madeiran archipelago; of greater interest to children is the spring-fed pond at the cave entrance, with its rainbow trout and ducklings.

🏛 48D3 ⊠ Sítio do Pé do Passo, São Vicente ☎ 842 404 ⏰ Apr–Sep, daily 9–9; Oct–Mar, daily 9–7 ♿ None 🍴 Expensive ➡ São Vicente (➤ 56)

Helicopter Trips

Taking to the sky is rather an extravagance, perhaps, but if you have money to spare and teenage children to treat, the ultimate in excursions is a helicopter trip over the mountains or along Madeira's scenic coastline.

Flights as short as 10 minutes can be arranged through any travel agent or through HeliAtlantis, Estrada da Pontinha, Cais de Contentores (☎ 232 882/4).

Jeep Safaris

Quite a number of Madeira's more spectacular mountain roads are as yet unmetalled (though there are long-term plans to upgrade them). While impassable to ordinary vehicles, they can be explored by jeep safari, which gives children the sense of being pioneers and explorers of virgin territory.

Bookings can be made through any travel agency, or through Terras de Aventura, Caminho do Amparo 25 (☎ 776 818).

Levada walking

If you do not feel confident about *levada* walking with children on your own, let experienced guides show you the way. Various walks are on offer from Turismo Verde e Ecológico da Madeira (☎ 766 109). Other companies offering similar walks are Natura (☎ 236 015; website: www.madeirawalks.com) and Nature Meetings (☎ 200 618; website: www.naturemeetings.com).

Teleféricos da Madeiras

For children who have been on a ski lift and are not afraid of heights, an enjoyable trip is the cable-car ride from the Old Town in Funchal up to the hill village of Monte.

Thanks to Austrian technology, you can be whisked above rooftops and ravines with intimate views of gardens and terraces, to the upper station, just below Monte's church, a journey of just over 10 minutes.

Once in Monte, the Monte Palace Tropical Gardens will keep children amused for a good hour or more with its eccentric mix of gardens, statuary, cascades and ponds (complete with ducks and huge koi carp). There are also grottoes and tunnels to explore. The round trip by cable car and the admission to the gardens adds up to quite an expensive day – but it is worth it if it keeps the children happy.

⊠ Caminho das Babosas 8, Monte; Avenida das Comunidades Madeirenses, Funchal ☎ 780 280; ⏰ Summer, daily 9–8:30. Winter, daily 9–6:30

Lido Complex

If your own hotel does not have an adequate pool, the municipal Lido Complex, in the Hotel Zone, is the perfect alternative. The complex includes an Olympic-sized main pool, a separate children's pool, access to the sea from a diving platform and a choice of places to eat. At weekends the complex can be crowded, but less so during week.

⊠ Rua do Gargulho ⏰ Apr–Sep, daily 8:30–7; Oct–Mar, daily 9–6

111

Sports

Quinta do Magnólia

The elegant Quinta do Magnólia was built as the British Country Club but now belongs to the Madeiran regional government. The former clubhouse, an elegant building with shady verandas, is now Madeira's Hotel and Tourism School. Pretty gardens surround the building and, for those in search of exercise, there is a full range of sports facilities, including tennis courts, a large swimming pool, a putting course, squash courts and a jogging track. Entrance is free, and bookings to use the squash and tennis courts should be made at the gatekeeper's lodge at the entrance.

Diving

Atalaia Diving

Atalaia Diving is one of three long-established diving clubs on Madeira. Operating out of Caniço, it offers a beginners course leading to the CMAS Bronze qualification, and a varied programme of dives at sites around the island.

✉ **Caniço** ☎ **934 330**

Dive College International

Fully trained and certified instructors offering courses and dives for beginners and experienced divers.

✉ **Hotel Dom Pedro Baia, Machico** ☎ **965 751**

Scorpio Divers

Another long-established diving club offering training courses for beginners, and a varied programme of dives for more experienced divers. Scorpio operates out of the Lido Complex, in Funchal's Hotel Zone, but also offers dives on Porto Santo during the summer season.

✉ **Complexo do Lido, Funchal** ☎ **66977**

Fishing

Madeira Big Game Fishing

Specialists in charter boats for sport fishing, Madeira Fishing offers four- or eight-hour trips for up to eight people.

✉ **Funchal Marina** ☎ **227 169; website: www.madeiragamefish.com**

Turispeca

Established more than 30 years ago, Turispeca specialises in big-game fishing trips for beginners and experienced anglers. Charters can be for between four and seven hours, and the price includes all necessary tackle and bait for up to five anglers. The experienced crews know where to go for the best fishing grounds; depending on the time of year, there are big blue marlin, big-eye tuna, blue-fin tuna, yellow-fin tuna, and various sharks to catch.

✉ **Yachting Marina, Funchal** ☎ **231 063**

Golf

Madeira Golf

The 27-hole Madeira Golf Club is set among the wooded hills of Santo da Serra, to whose cool heights wealthy Madeiran merchants used to retreat in the summer. Reservations can be made from most hotels (48 hours notice is recommended) and transport can be arranged from central Funchal. Equipment can be hired and you can attend the regular golf clinics, as well as booking private lessons.

✉ **Santo da Serra** ☎ **552 345**

Quinta do Palheiro Golf Club

The beautifully wooded and landscaped grounds of the Quinta do Palheiro estate were laid out in the late 18th century by a French gardener working for a wealthy Portuguese aristocrat, the Conde de Carvalhal. Today, part of the estate has been turned into a golf course, renowned for its scenic beauty. The clubhouse, built in traditional Madeiran style, enjoys fine views over Funchal. The 18-hole course, designed by Cabell Robinson, is a challenging medium-length course of 6,105m, set

among 100-year-old pine forest and lush native woodland, with views to the eastern end of the island.

✉ **Quinta do Palheiro**
☎ **792 116; website:**
www.madeira-golf.com

Health Clubs

Massage, aromatherapy, mud-wraps and facials – not exactly sports but a popular and growing holiday activity on Madeira. If you feel like being pampered, try the Essentially Natural Health Centre (☎ 706 280 ext. 2067) at the Vila Ramos Hotel, or the Thalassothys Spa, at the Dorisol Hotel (☎ 702 118).

Horse Riding

Club Ipismo

Catering both for beginners and experienced riders, the Club Ipismo offers the chance to explore hidden parts of Madeira from the back of a horse – more environmentally friendly by far than a jeep safari. Bookings can be made direct, or through the Hotel Estrelícia (☎ 706 600).
✉ **Caminho dos Pretos, Funchal** ☎ **224 982**

Motorsports

Madeira Wine Rally

The ear-ripping sound of high performance engines accelerating through the streets of central Funchal signals the start of the Madeira Wine Rally, regarded as one of the toughest stages in the European rallying champion-ship. The rally takes place during the first week in August. Visitors may find certain roads closed during the rally, especially to the west of the island; the rally route centres around the flat Paul da Serra plateau between Funchal and Porto do Moniz. You can watch the start and finish of the daily stages in Avenida Arriaga, in central Funchal. All the nearby bars will be full of macho Funchalese, watching the race on television and boasting of their own driving prowess.

Swimming

Because Maderia lacks classic and sand sea beaches, the luxury hotels of the hotel district have all invested in high-quality swimming facilities, most of which are open to non-residents for a small fee, which is often waived if you use the hotel's café or dining room.

Madeira also has some excellent public pools which are under-used outside the main summer season and weekends, so you'll probably enjoy as much privacy as in a private hotel pool. The biggest complex is the Lido, on Rua Gorgulho, in the Hotel Zone (☎ 231 150). Further out of Funchal is the Clube Naval do Funchal (✉ Estrada Pontinha ☎ 661 224), a civilised spot with pools, sea bathing and a café, open to anyone but kept more exclusive by costing three times as much as the Lido.

Tennis and Squash

Quinta do Magnólia
▶ 112, side panel.
✉ **Rua Dr Pita** ☎ **764 598**
🕐 **Daily 7:30AM–9PM**

Beneath the Waves
Anyone diving off Madeira can expect to see a good range of marine life in the island's clear waters and rocky foreshores. Of the big fish, the majestic manta rays are the most common; these gregarious fish seem to know when divers are about and you can be fairly sure that they will be along to play. Black crabs, the colour of the island's volcanic rocks, are common, as are sea anemones. With luck you may see a coral-coloured scorpion fish or a bright red parrot fish, so-called because of the shape of its beak-like mouth, which is used for prising limpets off the rocks.

Nightlife

Madeiran Dance
Madeira's traditional dance reflects the burdens of rural patterns of work. In the Carrier's Dance, the dancers bend beneath the weight of the imaginary stacks of sugar cane or baskets of bananas they carry along the island's steep paths. In the Heavy Dance, the rhythmic stamping of the dancers' feet reflects the custom of crushing grapes for wine with bare feet.

Cabaret

Carlton Park Hotel
It would be hard to better the Carlton Park Hotel for evening entertainment. As well as dinner dances with live acts in the restaurant, the next-door casino offers three different dinner shows. Choose between New York, New York, featuring song and dance routines from various Broadway musicals, Brazil Latino, with its hot rhythms and colourful fast-paced dancing, and the Cabaret Festival, an evening of extravagant dance, music and magic.
✉ **Rua Imperatriz Dona Amélia, Funchal** ☎ **231 121**
🕐 **All year**

Casinos

Casino da Madeira
Resembling a volcanic cone – or a rack of lamb, as the locals would have it – the Casino in Funchal is a striking building, designed by Oscar Niemeyer, the architect who created the master plan for the futuristic Brazilian capital, Brasília. The main gambling room has French and American roulette, Black Jack, French Bank and *chemin-de-fer* tables, and the entrance area is equipped with a range of slot machines. Located within the same complex are the Panoramic restaurant, with its floor show, and the Baccará discotheque. Entrance to the casino is restricted to those aged 18 and over, so passports are required as proof of age.
✉ **Avenida do Infante, Funchal** ☎ **231 121** 🕐 **Tue–Sat 9PM–4AM**

Cinema

Cinemax Cinema
Funchal's main cinema shows films in their original language with Portuguese subtitles.
✉ **Avenida Arriaga, Funchal**
☎ **231 933**
🕐 **Screenings daily at 2, 4:30, 7, 9:30**

Classical Music
Funchal has a thriving musical *conservatoire*, and you may be fortunate enough to catch a concert by students and teachers during your stay. Many of them are organised under the aegis of the Orquestra Clássica da Madeira (☎ 742 793). Ask at the Tourist Office for details of forthcoming events or look for posters around town.

Discos

O Farol
Packed during the summer, when top disc jockeys are brought over from mainland Portugal to entertain the holidaying Lisbonites. Quieter and mainly patronised by more affluent oldies during the rest of the year, when top hits of the 1960s are the most popular numbers.
✉ **Madeira Carlton Hotel, Largo António Nobre** ☎ **231 031** 🕐 **Daily 9:30PM–3AM**

Vespas
Vespas has been around for decades and remains everyone's favourite disco on Madeira. It now features a laser show.
✉ **Avenida Sa Carneiro, Funchal** ☎ **234 800** 🕐 **Daily midnight–6AM**

Folk Dancing and Music

Just about every hotel on Madeira offers folk-dancing evenings, and you can enjoy the same spectacle if you dine in the seafood restaurants lining the Yachting Marina in Funchal. At the best shows (such as that at the Café Relógio ► below), the dancers and musicians will explain the origins and history of their dances, instruments and costumes. Folk dancing on Madeira remains genuinely rooted in popular culture and there are numerous folklore groups around the island who perform at local festivals.

Café Relógio

Camacha is the base for one of Madeira's most accomplished folklore groups, and they can be seen in performance nightly at the Café Relógio's Panorama restaurant.

✉ **Camacha** ☎ **922 777**
⏰ **7–11PM**

Hotel-based Entertainment

To keep their clients happy, all the major hotels in Funchal's Hotel Zone have entertainment programmes that are also open to non-residents. They range from the ubiquitous Madeiran folk-dancing evenings to themed nights featuring the food and music of, say, France, Spain or Brazil. Noticeboards advertise forthcoming events.

Live Music

Arsénio's

The plaintive style of music known as *fado* (fate) is as popular on Madeira as it is in the back streets of Lisbon, where the style was originally born. Arsénio's is a good place to go to hear the music performed live as it has a long-established reputation for the quality of the singers and guitarists and it brings over to perform from the mainland.

✉ **Rua de Santa Maria 169, Funchal** ☎ **224 007**
⏰ **Daily noon–2AM**

Marcelino Fado House

If Arsénio's is full or you want to ring the changes, try the newer Marcelino Fado House for bar snacks and wine accompanied by soulful singing and guitar playing.

✉ **Travessa da Torre 22A, Funchal** ☎ **220 216**
⏰ **Daily 8:30PM–4AM**

Nightclubs

O Fugitivo

Energetic and scantily clad dancers from England and Brazil provide the entertainment at a venue that describes itself as a 'dancing pub'.

✉ **Rua Imperatriz Dona Amélia 68, Funchal** ☎ **222 003**
⏰ **Shows at midnight, 1:30, 3:30AM**

Theatre

Teatro Baltazar Dias, Funchal's gem of a theatre (also known as the Teatro Municipal), is the focal point for the island's artistic and cultural life. There is a regular programme of concerts, dance, theatre (usually in Portuguese) and art film. Look out for events advertised outside the theatre on Avenida Arriaga.

Madeiran Music

Musical accompaniment to Madeiran dance is provided by an instrument similar to a ukulélé, known as the *braguinha*. Rhythm is provided by wooden castanets, called *castanholes*, and a notched stick, called a *raspadeira*, played like a washboard.

What's On When

Village Festivals

Village festivals are held on Madeira to celebrate the feast day of the local saint, to whom the parish church is dedicated, or some special event in the history of the village (such as the procession in Machico on 8 October in honour of the crucifix that survived the destruction of the local church). Feast days usually begin with a religious service, but, come evening, exploding firecrackers and clanging church bells announce the start of the secular festivities, with dancing to the local band.

January

Grand New Year Firework Show (starts midnight on 31 December): the New Year starts with a bang and much noisy blowing of ships' hooters at one of Europe's most spectacular public fireworks festivals.

Dia de Reis (6 January): the Day of the Kings, with its religious services, marks the end of the Christmas and New Year celebrations.

February

Carnival (four days before Ash Wednesday): *Carnival* is celebrated all over Madeira, but the costumed parades in Funchal are definitely the best. On the Saturday before Ash Wednesday bands accompany a costumed parade, with clowns, dancers and people in spectacular fancy dress. Three days later the so-called Local Parade includes satirical floats that poke fun at local politicians.

April

Flower Festival (second or third weekend): Funchal becomes a blaze of colour for this festival, when shops, houses and churches are all decorated with ribbons and flags, and children make a wall of flowers in Praça do Município. The climax is a parade through Funchal with bands and colourful floats.

June

Fins de Semana Musicais (all month) Musical Weekends: Madeira's music festival features guest musicians and talented students from the local *conservatoire* performing in the cathedral and the Teatro Baltazar Dias.

August

Feast of the Assumption (15 August): Madeira's biggest religious festival is celebrated with religious services by day and dancing, fireworks and feasting by night. Penitents visit the church at Monte to climb the steps on their knees.

September

Madeira Wine Festival (13–15 September): in Funchal and Câmara de Lobos, the completion of the wine harvest is celebrated with public demonstrations of wine-treading, local music and dance and wine tastings.

October

Festa da Macã (25–26 October): the Apple Festival in Camacha offers an opportunity to sample the apples grown around Camacha, and to enjoy local folk singing and dancing, made more enjoyable by glasses of cider and apple brandy.

November

Festa da Castanha (1 November): the chestnut harvest in Curral das Freiras provides an excuse to consume chestnuts in myriad forms.

December

Christmas Illuminations (from 8 December): the build-up to Christmas begins when the street illuminations are officially switched on by a local dignitary.

Christmas Cribs (from 16 December): the Portuguese tradition of building tableaux representing the crib continues in Funchal, and in many villages.

Practical Matters

Above: cotton
knitwear in folk-art
patterns.
Right: armfuls of
arums symbolise
Madeira's floral
splendours

TIME DIFFERENCES

GMT
12 noon

Portugal
12 noon

Germany
1PM

USA (NY)
7AM

Netherlands
1PM

Spain
1PM

BEFORE YOU GO

WHAT YOU NEED

		UK	Germany	USA	Netherlands	Spain
● Required ○ Suggested ▲ Not required	Some countries require a passport to remain valid for a minimum period (usually at least six months) beyond the date of entry – contact their consulate or embassy or your travel agent for details.					
Passport/National Identity Card		●	●	●	●	●
Visa (Regulations can change – check before your journey)		▲	▲	▲	▲	▲
Onward or Return Ticket		○	○	○	○	○
Health Inoculations		▲	▲	▲	▲	▲
Health Documentation (reciprocal agreement document ► 123, Health)		●	●	▲	●	●
Travel Insurance		○	○	○	○	○
Driving Licence (national with Portuguese translation or International)		●	●	●	●	●
Car Insurance Certificate (if own car)		●	●	●	●	●
Car Registration Document (if own car)		●	●	●	●	●

WHEN TO GO

Funchal

■ High season
□ Low season

18°C	19°C	19°C	20°C	21°C	22°C	24°C	25°C	25°C	23°C	22°C	19°C
JAN	FEB	MAR	APR	MAY	JUN	JUL	AUG	SEP	OCT	NOV	DEC

 Sun

 Sunshine & showers

TOURIST OFFICES

In the UK
Portuguese National Tourist Office
22–25A Sackville Street
London W1X 1DE
☎ 020 7494 5725
Fax: 020 7494 1868

In the USA
Portuguese National Tourist Office
590 Fifth Avenue, 4th Floor
New York
NY 10036
☎ 212/354 4403
Fax: 212/764 6137

POLICE 112

FIRE 112

AMBULANCE 112

WHEN YOU ARE THERE

ARRIVING

Cruise ships regularly call at Funchal on the way to the Caribbean, but most visitors to Madeira arrive by air. Santa Catarina airport is served by flights from most European airports, either direct or via Lisbon. TAP Air Portugal is the national airline (in Funchal ☎ 239 210; fax: 239 248).

Santa Catarina Airport Kilometres to city centre	**Journey times**	
	🚶	N/A
22 kilometres	🚌	50 minutes
	🚗	35 minutes

MONEY

Portugal's currency is the euro, which is divided into 100 cents. Coins come in denominations of 1, 2, 5, 10, 20 and 50 cents and 1 and 2 euros. Notes come in denominations of 5, 10, 20, 50, 100 and 500 euros (the last two are rarely seen). The notes and one side of the coins are the same throughout the European single currency zone. Notes and coins from any of the other countries in the zone can be used in Portugal.

Mastercard, Visa, American Express and Diners cards are widely accepted, as are travellers' cheques. Banks with exchange bureaux are found in Funchal and the larger towns. Commission on changing euro travellers' cheques can be high.

TIME

 Madeira, like mainland Portugal, observes Greenwich Mean Time during the winter months; during the summer, from late March to late September, the time is GMT plus 1 hour.

CUSTOMS

 YES

From another EU country for personal use (guidelines):
800 cigarettes, 200 cigars,
1 kilogram of tobacco
10 litres of spirits (over 22%)
20 litres of aperitifs
90 litres of wine, of which 60 litres can be sparkling wine
110 litres of beer

From a non-EU country for personal use:
200 cigarettes OR 50 cigars OR 250 grams of tobacco
1 litre of spirits (over 22%)
2 litres of intermediary products (eg sherry) and sparkling wine
2 litres of still wine
50 grams of perfume
0.25 litres of eau de toilette
The value limit for goods is 175 euros

Travellers under 17 are not entitled to the tobacco and alcohol allowances.

 NO

Narcotic drugs, firearms, ammunition, offensive weapons, obscene material, unlicensed animals.

UK
☎ 221 221

Germany
☎ 220 338

USA
☎ 743 429

Netherlands
☎ 223 890

WHEN YOU ARE THERE

TOURIST OFFICES

Funchal
- Avenida Arriaga 16
  ☎ 225 658
  Fax: 232 151
  E-mail: info@madeira-tourism.org

Machico
- Forte de Nossa Senhora do Amparo
  ☎ 962 289

Porto Santo
- Rua Dr Vieira da Castro
  ☎ 982 361

Ribeira Brava
- Forte de São Bento
  ☎ 951 675

Santana
- Sítio do Serrado
  ☎ 572 992

Some travel agencies in Funchal advertise themselves as if they were tourist information centres, though their primary aim is to sell you one of their organised tours. In general these tours (by mini bus or coach) are good value and the standards of safety are high. You must expect, however, that the tour will include time spent in shops and restaurants rather than sightseeing – you may prefer to have the flexibility of your own taxi with driver, which can work out as cheap as an organised tour if three or four people share a car.

NATIONAL HOLIDAYS

J	F	M	A	M	J	J	A	S	O	N	D
1	1	(1)	2	1	2	1	2		1	1	4

1 Jan	New Year
Feb (dates vary)	Shrove Tuesday & Ash Wednesday
Mar/Apr	Good Friday, Easter Monday
25 Apr	Day of the Revolution
1 May	Labour Day
Jun (date varies)	Corpus Christi
10 Jun	National Day
1 Jul	Madeira Day
15 Aug	Feast of the Assumption
21 Aug	Funchal Day
5 Oct	Republic Day
1 Nov	All Saints' Day
1 Dec	Restoration of Independence Day
8 Dec	Immaculate Conception
25/26 Dec	Christmas

OPENING HOURS

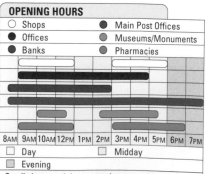

○ Shops	● Main Post Offices
● Offices	◐ Museums/Monuments
● Banks	◐ Pharmacies

8AM 9AM 10AM 12PM 1PM 2PM 3PM 4PM 5PM 6PM 7PM

☐ Day	☐ Midday
☐ Evening	

Small shops and those catering to tourists are open daily from around 8AM until 7 or 8PM, including Sundays and public holidays. Larger stores and supermarkets increasingly ignore the lunch break and are open continuously from 9–7. Some supermarkets stay open until 10 (5 on Sunday). Pharmacies open late on a duty rota (posted on pharmacy doors). Village post offices have shorter opening hours; main post offices also open Saturday morning.

**DRIVE ON THE
RIGHT**

**TOILETS
FREE**

PUBLIC TRANSPORT

Internal Flights There are several flights a day from Funchal to Porto Santo. The 37km journey takes 15 minutes, and flights are heavily booked in high season, so be sure to book well in advance. Flights can be booked through any travel agent or through branches of TAP Air Portugal. On Madeira TAP's office is at Avenida das Comunidades Madeirenses 10 (☎ 239 210).

Buses A highly efficient bus system connects all towns with Funchal. Buses are modern and comfortable (though they do not have safety belts) and most drivers take care to drive safely on Madeira's tortuous roads. Buses within Funchal and its suburbs are painted orange; those serving the rural areas are operated by five different companies, each with its own livery. Nearly all buses depart from the bus stops along Avenida do Mar, where you can also buy tickets from the bus company kiosks (7-day go-as-you-please passes are available to visitors only, so bring your passport if you want to buy one). Up-to-date timetables are available from the Tourist Office on Avenida Arriaga 18.

Boat Trips The *Lobo Marinho* ferry, serving Porto Santo, departs from the pier (*pontinha*) next to the yachting marina in Funchal at 8AM daily (except Tuesday). Tickets can be bought in advance from travel agents, or from the pier just before sailing. Further information from their Porto Santo Line, Rua da Praia 4, Funchal (☎ 210 300). A number of cruise companies operate out of Funchal's yachting marina, all offering half- or full-day excursions around Madeira's coastline. Turispeca (☎ 231 063) operates charter cruises, game-fishing trips and regular cruises (including evening cruises with dinner).

CAR RENTAL

The major car rental firms are represented on Madeira, as well as several local companies, which offer competitive rates. You can book a car in advance through travel agents, at the airport on arrival or through your hotel. All rental firms will deliver your car to you.

TAXIS

There are taxi ranks in towns and taxis may also stop if flagged down, especially in the countryside. Rates for out-of-town journeys (eg from Funchal to the airport) are fixed. Short journeys are metered. For longer journeys, you can negotiate an hourly or half-day rate.

DRIVING

Speed limit on motorways: **110kph**

Speed limit on main roads: **80kph**

Speed limit on urban roads: **60 or 40kph**

It is mandatory for drivers and passengers to wear seat belts if fitted.

Breath Testing: random tests are carried out.

Petrol (*gasolina*) comes in two grades: lead-free (*sem chumbo*) and lead-substitute (*super*). Diesel (*gasóleo*) is also available. Most villages and towns have a petrol station, and they are generally open from 8 to 8. The GALP petrol station on Avenida do Infante, in Funchal, is open 24 hours. Most take credit cards.

Because all visitors to Madeira drive rental cars, there is no central breakdown and rescue service. Instead, the car rental companies operate their own breakdown services, with repairs usually being carried out promptly. The documents you are given on hiring the car will explain what to do in the event of a breakdown.

PERSONAL SAFETY

Crime on Madeira is extremely rare. In the unlikely event that you are the victim of theft, report your loss to the main police station at the Rua Dr João de Deus 7 (☎ 222 022) and get a copy of the written statement in order to support your insurance claim.

- Leave your valuables in the hotel.
- Do not leave valuables in cars.
- Do not leave unattended valuables on the beach or poolside.
- Beware of pickpockets in markets and on crowded streets.

Police assistance:
☎ **112**
from any call box

TELEPHONES

Telephones are found in cafés and on the streets of larger towns. Some only take phonecards, available from newsagents and cafés. To call Madeira or Porto Santo from abroad dial 00 351 (the international code for Portugal) then 291 (the area code for both islands). In Madeira and Porto Santo you only need to dial the subscriber number.

International Dialling Codes From Madeira (Portugal) to:	
UK:	00 44
Germany:	00 49
USA and Canada:	00 1
Netherlands:	00 31
Spain:	00 34

POST

Post Offices
Post offices (*Correios*) are found in the main towns. In Funchal, the most central post office is on Avenida do Zarco. Poste restante services are available at the main post office on Rua Dr Joao Brito Camara. Stamps can also be bought from many newsagents. Open: Mon–Fri 8:30–8, Sat 9–12:30

ELECTRICITY

The power supply on Madeira is:
220 volts AC.

Sockets accept continental two-pronged plugs, so an adaptor is needed for non-continental appliances, and a transformer for devices operating on 100–120 volts.

TIPS/GRATUITIES

Yes ✓ No ✗		
Tipping is appreciated but not required on Madeira.		
Restaurants (service and tax included)	✓	10%
Bar service	✓	change
Taxis	✓	10%
Tour guides	✓	€1.50
Chambermaids	✗	No
Swimming pool attendants	✓	change
Porters	✓	€1.50
Hairdressers	✓	10%
Toilets	✗	No

PHOTOGRAPHY
What to photograph: Madeira's mountainous landscape will provide you with many subjects, including waterfalls, sheer cliffs, volcanic landscapes and deep ravines. For colour, there are markets, flowers and traditional costumes.
Best time to photograph: the light is best before 10AM, after which time you can expect haze and clouds. Madeira's sunsets are brief but colourful.
Where to buy film: most hotels sell film and batteries, and there are several specialist photo shops, also offering processing services, in central Funchal.

HEALTH

Insurance
Nationals of EU countries receive free emergency medical treatment on Madeira with the relevant documentation (form E111 for UK nationals), although private medical insurance is still advised and is essential for all other visitors.

Dental Services
Dental services on Madeira are excellent. Dentists advertise their services in the free English- and German-language magazines that are available from most hotels and the tourist information centre in Funchal.

Sun Advice
The sun can be intense on Madeira at any time of the year, and it is possible to burn with less than an hour's exposure. If you are out walking on bare mountains, it is best to cover vulnerable parts of your body, including your neck, legs and arms.

Drugs
Chemists (*farmácia*) are open Mon–Fri 9–1 and 3–7, and Sat 9–12:30. Some open through the lunch break, and there is a late-night duty rota, posted in pharmacy windows. Take supplies of any drugs that you take regularly, since there is no guarantee that they will be available locally.

Safe Water
Tap water is safe to drink everywhere. The water is fresh and often comes straight from pure mountain springs. Mineral water is available everywhere; if you ask for fizzy water (*água com gás*), rather than still (*água sem gás*), it is likely to be naturally sparkling, rather than carbonated.

CONCESSIONS

Students/youths: Museums have lower rates of admission for students, and entry is free for children. Bring a passport or student card as proof of your age.
Senior Citizens: Many senior citizens come to Madeira for the winter months, attracted by warm weather, a low cost of living and heavily discounted low-season long-stay rates. Ask travel agents specialising in Madeira for details.

CLOTHING SIZES

Madeira	UK	Rest of Europe	USA		
46	36	46	36		
48	38	48	38		
50	40	50	40		
52	42	52	42		Suits
54	44	54	44		
56	46	56	46		
41	7	41	8		
42	7.5	42	8.5		
43	8.5	43	9.5		
44	9.5	44	10.5		Shoes
45	10.5	45	11.5		
46	11	46	12		
37	14.5	37	14.5		
38	15	38	15		
39/40	15.5	39/40	15.5		
41	16	41	16		Shirts
42	16.5	42	16.5		
43	17	43	17		
34	8	34	6		
36	10	36	8		
38	12	38	10		
40	14	40	12		Dresses
42	16	42	14		
44	18	44	16		
38	4.5	38	6		
38	5	38	6.5		
39	5.5	39	7		
39	6	39	7.5		Shoes
40	6.5	40	8		
41	7	41	8.5		

WHEN DEPARTING

- Funchal airport is small and does not have extensive shopping facilities.
- High winds can occasionally disrupt flights into and out of Madeira, in which case incoming flights are diverted to Porto Santo, and outgoing flights are delayed. Late October/early November are the riskiest periods.
- You are advised to arrive at the airport no later than one hour before the departure time.

LANGUAGE

Portuguese is the language of Madeira, but most hoteliers, shopkeepers and restaurateurs speak English and German as well. Portuguese is easy to understand in its written form if you already know a Romance language – such as Latin, French, Italian or Spanish. When pronounced, however, it could easily be mistaken for a Slavic language. Two sounds are distinctive to Portuguese: vowels accented with a tilde sound like *owoo* (so bread, *pão*, is pronounced *powoo*) and the s and z, which are pronounced *zsh* (so *carros*, car, is pronounced *carrozsh*).

hotel	*hotel/estalagem*	double room	*quarto de casal*
do you have a room?	*tem um quarto livre?*	twin room	*quarto com duas camas*
I have a reservation	*tenho um quarto reservado*	with bathroom	*com banho*
how much per night?	*qual e o preço por noite?*	one night	*um noite*
		key	*chave*
a single room	*um quarto simples*	sea view	*vista a mar*
		gents/ladies	*senhores/senhoras*

bank	*um banco*	pounds/dollars	*libras/dólares*
exchange office	*câmbios*	do you take?	*aceitam?*
post office	*correio*	credit card	*cartão de crédito*
coins	*moedas*		
banknotes	*notas*	traveller's cheque	*cheque de viagem*
receipt	*recibo*		
the change	*troco*	cheque	*cheque*
can you change?	*pode trocar?*	how much?	*quanta custa?*

breakfast	*pequeno almoço*	beer	*cerveja*
lunch	*almoço*	menu	*lista*
dinner	*jontar*	red wine	*vinho tinto*
table	*mesa*	white wine	*vinho branco*
starter	*entrada*	water	*água*
main course	*prato principal*	tea	*chà*
dessert	*sobremesa*	coffee (black)	*um bica*
bill	*conta*	coffee (white)	*café con leite*

airport	*aeroporto*	which way to?	*como se vai para?*
bus	*autocarro*		
bus station	*estação de autocarros*	how far?	*a que distância?*
		where is?	*onde está?*
bus stop	*paragem*	car	*carro*
a ticket to	*um bilhete para*	petrol	*gasolina*
single	*ida*	petrol station	*posto de gasolina*
return	*ide e volta*		

yes	*sim*	good evening /night	*boa noite*
no	*não*		
please	*faz favor*	excuse me	*desculpe*
thank you (male)	*obrigado*	you're welcome	*está bem*
thank you (female)	*obrigada*	how are you?	*camo está?*
		well, thank you	*bem, obrigado (a)*
hello	*olá*	not at all	*de nada*
goodbye	*adeus*	do you speak English?	*fala inglês?*
good morning	*bom dia*		
good afternoon	*boa tarde*	I don't understand	*não compreendo*

INDEX

Acknowledgements

The Automobile Association wishes to thank the following photographers and libraries for their assistance in the preparation of this book.

MARY EVANS PICTURE LIBRARY 11b
www.euro.ecb.int/ (euro notes) 119
INTERNATIONAL PHOTOBANK 61b
PICTURES COLOUR LIBRARY 15b, 31, 34b, 54
PORTO SANTO DIVING CENTRE 69b
SPECTRUM COLOUR LIBRARY 18b, 117b
WORLD PICTURES LTD 2, 26b, 28/9, 56, 87, 88, 91b

The remaining photographs are held in the Association's own photo library (AA PHOTO LIBRARY) and were taken by JON WYAND, with the exception of the following: F/cover (a) Santana, thatched house, (b) Garajau, Statue of Christ, (c) Monte, tobbogan, and pages 6b, 27b, 39b, 42b, 42d, 45b, 57b, 62b, 68b, 74b, 76b, 77b, 78, 78/9, 81b, 83b, 122a, 122b which were taken by PETER BAKER; page 13b taken by TONY OLIVER, and F/cover (e) girl in costume, (f) Sé Cathedral, (g) wine barrel, bottom tile, B/cover Camera de Lobos and page 16b taken by CLIVE SAWYER.

Copy editor: Rebecca Snelling

Dear Essential Traveller

**Your comments, opinions and recommendations are very
important to us. So please help us to improve our travel
guides by taking a few minutes to complete this simple
questionnaire.**

*You do not need a stamp (unless posted outside the UK). If you do not want to cut this page
from your guide, then photocopy it or write your answers on a plain sheet of paper.*

Send to: **The Editor, AA World Travel Guides,
FREEPOST SCE 4598, Basingstoke RG21 4GY.**

Your recommendations...

We always encourage readers' recommendations for restaurants, nightlife
or shopping – if your recommendation is used in the next edition of the
guide, we will send you a *FREE* **AA** *Essential* **Guide** of your choice.
Please state below the establishment name, location and your reasons
for recommending it.

_____

_____

_____

_____

Please send me **AA** *Essential* _____

(*see list of titles inside the front cover*)

About this guide...

Which title did you buy?

AA *Essential* _____

Where did you buy it? _____

When? m m / y y

Why did you choose an AA *Essential* Guide? _____

_____

_____

_____

_____

Did this guide meet your expectations?

Exceeded ☐   Met all ☐   Met most ☐   Fell below ☐

Please give your reasons _____

_____

_____

_____

continued on next page...

Were there any aspects of this guide that you particularly liked? _____

_____

_____

_____

Is there anything we could have done better? _____

_____

_____

_____

_____

About you...

Name (*Mr/Mrs/Ms*) _____

Address _____

_____

_____ Postcode _____

Daytime tel nos _____

Which age group are you in?
Under 25 ☐   25–34 ☐   35–44 ☐   45–54 ☐   55–64 ☐   65+ ☐

How many trips do you make a year?
Less than one ☐   One ☐   Two ☐   Three or more ☐

Are you an AA member? Yes ☐   No ☐

About your trip...

When did you book? m m / y y   When did you travel? m m / y y
How long did you stay? _____
Was it for business or leisure? _____
Did you buy any other travel guides for your trip?
    If yes, which ones? _____

_____

Thank you for taking the time to complete this questionnaire. Please send
it to us as soon as possible, and remember, you do not need a stamp
(*unless posted outside the UK*).

Happy Holidays!